U.S. International Broadcasting and National Security

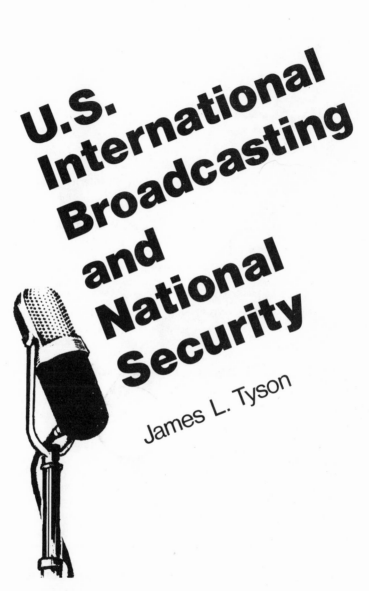

James L. Tyson

RAMAPO Press

National Strategy Information Center, Inc.

**U.S. International Broadcasting
and National Security**

Published in the United States by

Ramapo Press
363 Seventh Avenue
New York, NY 10001

Copyright © 1983 National Strategy Information Center, Inc.
150 East 58th Street
New York, NY 10155

Library of Congress Cataloging in Publication Data

Tyson, James L.
U.S. international broadcasting and national security.

Includes bibliographical references.
1. Voice of America (Radio Program)—History. 2. Radio
Free Europe—History. 3. Radio Liberty (Munich, Germany)
—History. 4. International broadcasting—History.
I. Title.

HE8698.T97 1983   384.54'53   83-22996
ISBN 0-915071-00-2

Printed in the United States of America

Table of Contents

Preface

Radio is more American than apple pie. Any baker or restauranteur will tell you that by no means does every American like apple pie. But what home is without its radio, or two or more? What car, beach or bar isn't part of the audience? Whatever gripe about this program or that, radio is a generic part of life that no American would dream of challenging.

Not so beyond the water's edge. Blue jeans, cola, movies, and other artifacts of American culture have streamed into countries all over the world, with few objections here. Commercial TV and radio programs are exported for reairing. Any qualms about the unflattering image some project are quickly shrugged off. That's entertainment! But when radio gets into the serious business of international politics, the objections come thick and fast.

The reasons for such diffidence, of course, are eminently healthy. Free people in a free society are instinctively hostile to anything smacking of a "Ministry of Information," even when it is directed against adversary powers that wish us no well. "Propaganda" is a dirty word, something fit only for totalitarians. A nation that maintains the most formidable ar-

senals of arms, from rifles to nuclear missiles, is suddenly
tongue-tied about employing words.

Yet, as James Tyson recounts in this study, overseas radio
has operated from these shores for over forty years. It went to
war with General Eisenhower's troops in North Africa and Europe, and with the civilian Office of War Information's Voice
of America. Psychological warfare supplemented the bombers
and landing craft, as the VOA buttressed President Roosevelt's
diplomacy. War overrode inhibition in this instance, as it did
in so many others.

V-J Day was the signal to pull all the switches. "Peace" had
returned, the opposite of "war." The war aims had been
achieved, and it was time to go home. In peace, there was no
need for clandestine services. In fact, psychological warfare or
large armed forces were considered provocative and inconsistent with a free people's behavior.

Of all the wartime innovations, VOA was among the few
to survive, barely. The Office of Strategic Services was abolished. Psychological warfare was relegated to a tiny record-
keeping detachment at the old Indian War post, Fort Riley,
Kansas. It reappeared briefly in the Korean War, then almost
disappeared as the "Psychological Operations" arm of "Special
Forces." "Warfare" was too strong a potion to survive in
"peacetime." In the view of many, in Congress and out, so was
the "Voice of America."

What kept VOA alive, as Mr. Tyson tells it, was not so much
argument as events. "Peace" rapidly proved to be Cold War
— "Neither peace nor war," to use Trotsky's aphorism. In the
face of massive and well-funded Soviet propaganda, the need
for something like VOA was almost self-evident. The United
States had either to cede that part of the conflict or answer in
kind. Not only did VOA remain, but three new efforts had to
be added: Radio in the American Sector, Berlin, Radio Free
Europe, and Radio Liberation. Cold War was detestable,
in many American eyes, but in many more it had to be waged,
just as hot war could not always be avoided by refusing to face
it.

The critics have never been converted, and their points have
been sound, as far as they went: Is there a "Voice" for a nation

that has many voices? Might not broadcasting put this country into the position of making promises that policy cannot redeem? Can "information" stay pure of "propaganda?" Indeed, does it really have an effect, and if so, is it the one desired?

Even as the merits of these questions have been debated, the record has provided working answers: There has been *a* Voice, though it has sounded differently at different times. Broadcasts must not promise what cannot be delivered, and after early false starts, have not. Information can exclude the blatant abuses of truth practiced by others, but there is a strategic case for selectivity in content. And, hard as it is to measure, there is an effect, as people in the audience areas have testified repeatedly.

The Radios are still high on the public policy agenda. The debate about their mission and structure, far from slackening, is fueled by the deep changes that have taken place within the U.S.-Soviet conflict itself. America's nuclear superiority, unchallengeable when the Radios were born, has vanished. In addition, the confrontation points between U.S. and Soviet interests are no longer confined to Europe, but are truly global. There are also rising questions in this country about its ability to apply its armed power at those points, and indeed whether or not that power is properly designed for such tasks.

In these circumstances, attention is forced to the other weapons in the spectrum, such as radio. Cold analysis of adversary capabilities and vulnerabilities imposes the conclusion that the populations of the U.S.S.R. and its captive states are a prime target. Communicating with those populations is not just a matter of compassion for their plight but a practical necessity in light of the conflict that won't go away and could become worse. The Soviets depend on those populations to support their strategic goals and to provide much of the combat strength. They are also, by the same token, the weak links in the Soviet armor. Radio is the prime way of reaching them.

Mr. Tyson's recommendations are based on the assumption that, first, they can be reached and, second, that they must be reached in this neither–war–nor–peace period. The second assumption can be quarreled with, but there is a choice to be made, and the record comes down on the side of that assumption. If so, there is much to be done to step up the management, structure and effectiveness of the Radios.

One of the most troubling problems is what to tell the American public about the Radios, and how. Almost alone among the non–classified operations of the Government, the Radios are highly restricted in informing their sponsors about what they are doing, and why. The responsible committees of Congress are informed, of course, but the appeals that other agencies routinely make are denied to the Radios.

The reason, again, is convincing: the public must not be propagandized by official and quasi-official media. But to keep government from telling the people what the Radios are saying is less convincing. Government in a democracy is obliged to promote its activities, as well as conduct them. The effect of keeping the public largely in the dark about any non–secret activity of this scope, therefore, is to leave the information conflict to too few hands, advocates as well as opponents. Just as defense is too important to leave to the generals, or welfare to the case workers, information is too important to leave to its "experts."

Some of the needed balance is restored by private–sector efforts like Mr. Tyson's. It bridges information and national security, conceptualizing for concerned readers what the historical record reveals about the connection between the two. Agree with his conclusions and recommendations or not, the facts upon which they are based must be known and faced.

October 1983

Gerald L. Steibel
Vice President and
Director of Studies,
National Strategy
Information Center, Inc.

Introduction

American international broadcasting strategy has been the subject of growing attention and debate in the government, Congress, and the media over the last two years. The policies of the Voice of America and Radio Free Europe/Radio Liberty have been widely covered by frequent media reports, interviews, and letters to the editor.

The subject of American broadcasting policy warrants such attention for several reasons. There is a Soviet military/strategic challenge to the West which has been increasing over the past decade. Differences of opinion may arise over appropriate responses to that challenge, but there is significant sentiment in official Washington which suggests that international broadcasting, if properly administered, can be one of the most cost-effective arms of foreign policy. In fiscal year 1982, for example, the total cost of U.S. broadcasting efforts amounted to less than $200 million, the approximate cost of one B-1 bomber.[1]

At the same time, many observers believe that the Soviets regard such broadcasting and other information from the West as one of the most serious ideological challenges to their regime. It is clear that the Kremlin does not expect a military invasion or attack from the West, in spite of Soviet propaganda to the contrary. But Western radio broadcasts into Soviet and Warsaw Pact territories, reaching their citizens daily, are regarded as a constant threat to Soviet political authority and stability.[2]

The Soviets devote massive resources to jamming Western radio broadcasts, an effort that costs fifty percent more than the total cost of all American international broadcasting.[3] But a substantial amount of Western radio transmissions still reaches East bloc audiences.

Another reason for the importance of this subject is the general agreement by many observers that America's international broadcasting capability has seriously deteriorated over the past decade. These observers include members of both parties in Congress who concern themselves with radio policy, and officials of the present administration responsible for international communications. Officers of the American radios have been testifying with increasing concern in recent years about the systematic decline in both physical equipment and manpower availability. Real dollar budgets as well as manpower levels in the broadcasting field have not increased appreciably for the past ten years. The present broadcasting effort is small compared to the Soviet enterprise. The budgets for the Voice of America and RFE/RL at around $200 million compare with over $700 million spent by the U.S.S.R. for broadcasting, and an estimated $300 million more for jamming.[4]

In part, the Soviets are using these huge resources to beam propaganda outside the U.S.S.R. But Soviet propagandists also have been engaged in a massive internal indoctrination effort ever since the Bolshevik Revolution. There are no concrete estimates of the cost of this internal program, but a conception of its size can be inferred from the figures on the number of people involved. According to data in *Pravda* and other publications, there are more than 1.5 million "agit-props" working full-time and another 5 million part-time in the Soviet internal propaganda organizations.[5]

This extensive effort purveys a line that rejects past American attempts to conduct a more constructive relationship with the government and people of the Soviet Union. In fact, Soviet domestic propaganda, contrary to many of the pronouncements for foreign consumption, transmits messages in favor of protracted struggle against capitalism and the Western democracies. Some of the main themes of the propaganda can be summarized as follows:

(1) The U.S.S.R. is faced with increasing military threats from the bourgeois capitalist powers. The Soviet people should redouble their efforts through massive arms and training programs to protect the Soviet Union from the growing aggressive intentions of the West. In fact, American analysts of Soviet propaganda output contend that the buildup of a mass war psychology is more explicit now than during any previous period in Soviet history, including even the years before the Nazi invasion.

(2) The Western powers are ruled by bourgeois regimes that oppress the working class. A capitalist "free" press is simply a vehicle for avaricious publishers to assist the ruling class in manipulating the masses.

(3) Any apparent economic prosperity of the democracies is due to the imperialist exploitation of the Third World, taking advantage of the raw materials and inexpensive labor available in the underdeveloped nations.

(4) The class struggle continues around the world, as does the struggle between the capitalists countries ruled by the bourgeoisie and the socialist countries.[6]

Such propaganda platforms have considerable influence on the people of the Soviet Union, and some effect in the Eastern European countries. Even though these people are to a great extent disillusioned with Marxist-Leninist ideology and practice, large numbers are not yet convinced that life in the Western democracies is better. Soviet propaganda efforts have complicated Western broadcasting programs in the past, particularly in that such a massive undertaking makes it more difficult to create any popular pressure on the Soviet leadership to negotiate seriously for arms reductions. Similarly, pervasive Soviet propaganda pressures the men and women in the armed forces of the Soviet bloc to believe sincerely in the virtues of preserving "socialism," even if they have to invade their neighbors to do so. There have been reports of Soviet soldiers being astonished to find that, upon invading Hungary or Czechoslovakia, they were greeted with hatred rather than being welcomed as liberators. As Alexandr Solzhenitsyn said, Western radio and other messages are important in reaching the soldiers of the communist armed forces to educate them to the fact that when Soviet generals send them into other nations, they will be looked upon not as liberators, but as conquerors.[7]

While there is an increasing consensus that the budgets and the physical plant of the American broadcasting organs are inadequate, most of the debate has arisen in the past few years over the content of the radio programs. Should there be an explicit attempt to counter or refute Soviet propaganda? Should American broadcasting programs include an articulation of American foreign policy and an effort to impart to the listeners of the East bloc an alternative set of values to the communist system, an enunciation of the Western heritage? Or should American radio broadcasts confine themselves to the news and "objective" descriptions of American life?

Such questions are particularly important at this time with respect to the foreign and information policies of the present U.S. administration. The Reagan administration has launched a plan for a bipartisan and global effort to promote democracy in cooperation with other democratic countries. First announced in President Reagan's speech before the British Parliament in June 1982, this program would be a worldwide campaign to "foster the infrastructure of democracy" in countries now ruled by communist dictatorships. In October 1982, the State Department hosted a Conference on the Democratization of Communist Countries to pursue further ideas on this subject. Secretary of State George Shultz opened the meeting by saying that the United States has both "a moral and a strategic responsibility" to heed the calls for help of those desiring more freedom in communist countries. Should the Radios be utilized as one element in this program, to encourage nonviolent efforts by the people in the communist countries to reduce the power of the central government and to curtail their ability to follow aggressive foreign policies?

Whether or not they are employed for such specific purposes, will the American broadcasting organizations be given a new lease on life under the present administration, or will they be neglected and continue to decline and perhaps fade into insignificance?

This report will briefly outline the history of American international broadcasting in its relation to foreign policy and will describe several proposals for strengthening the effort in the future as it relates to American foreign policy. The focus will be mainly on broadcasting to the Soviet Union and Warsaw Pact countries, the field that has generated most of the discussion during the past few years. The last third of the study will outline historical conclusions and offer recommendations for upgrading America's broadcasting capabilities.

NOTES

1. See Appendix A for actual budgets for fiscal years 1981 and 1982.
2. John Lenczowski, "A Foreign Policy for Reaganauts," *Policy Review*, Fall 1981, p. 80.
3. Board for International Broadcasting, *1983 Annual Report*, (Washington, D.C.: U.S. Government Printing Office), p. 3.
4. USIA estimates quoted by Senator Charles Percy (R-Ill.), *Congressional Record*, December 16, 1982, p. S15103.
5. Full-time figures from *Pravda*, September 11, 1978. Part-time and total estimates from Professor A. F. Okulov, *Party Organization and Atheist Education* (Moscow: Politizdat), p. 13, furnished to author by the East European Bible Mission, Roosendahl, the Netherlands.
6. These themes are summarized from: Sergei Sabur, "Seriously About Liberty," *Kontinent*, October 1981 (translated by the Association of Friends of the Periodical *Kontinent*), p. 3; *Soviet World Outlook*, published by the Advanced International Studies Institute, issues for March through May, 1981, and August 1982 through January 1983.
7. *RFE/RL — A Year of Merger* (Washington, D.C.: RFE/RL Inc.), 1976, p. 5

Part I
HISTORY

1
World War II and the Origins of U.S. International Broadcasting

Present controversies over American international broadcasting policy can best be understood after a review of its history. Many of the issues under discussion in recent months are reminiscent of those raised in earlier years. The three principal U.S. international broadcasting organs, the Voice of America and Radio Free Europe/Radio Liberty, have each experienced periods in which various policies being recommended today were tested and subsequently either adopted or abandoned. Such fluctuations in broadcasting policies over the years have reflected the basic strains in foreign policy, just as current and future broadcasting policies will be strongly affected by present diplomatic conditions as well as our conception of American relationships with the U.S.S.R. and its satellites.

The history of the American international broadcasting to the Soviet bloc countries can be divided into roughly seven periods:

— *World War II. First American International Broadcasting:* VOA Founded.

— *1946. Holding Operation:* Most wartime agencies are disbanded; VOA barely survives due to the efforts of a few backers. American foreign policy is based on the premise that the Soviets may be mellowing and are sincerely interested in the "peaceful coexistence" that they advocate.

— *1947-52. Cold War, Hot War, and a Strong Voice:* Hopes for political cooperation with the Soviet Union dwindle. America launches policy of "containment," with some hopes for "liberation" or "rollback." VOA is revived and other broadcasting organs initiated (Radio Free Europe and Radio Liberation).

— *1953-60. Retrenchment and Revision of Mission:* Broadcasting remains anti-communist but becomes more constrained, "calm and persuasive." Liberation idea abandoned in both foreign policy community and broadcasting policy.

— *1961-63. Height of Material Support for Broadcasting:* Kennedy and Murrow establish broadcasting policy that is anti-communist but not "strident."

— *1964-80. Detente and Growing Controversies:* Downgrading of U.S. international broadcasting; increasing policy and personnel conflicts under the Johnson, Nixon, Ford, and Carter administrations.

— *1981 to Date: Detente in Doubt—Search for New Guidelines:* Reagan administration attempts to revive broadcasting as an arm of American foreign policy.

This report will describe these phases and outline in more detail how the changes in the international situation and American foreign policy brought about changes in broadcast policy.

America's first venture into international broadcasting was launched in 1940 after the Nazi victories in Europe, when the Roosevelt administration was becoming increasingly concerned about the effects of German propaganda in Latin America. In August 1940 an Executive Order established the

Office for Coordination of Commercial and Cultural Relations between the American Republics to promote the use of government and private radio broadcasting and other means of information throughout the Americas. In July 1941 Roosevelt authorized the formation of the Office of the Coordinator of Information, under Colonel William Donovan, to assume similar responsibilities for other parts of the world.[1]

Donovan appointed the noted playwright, Robert Sherwood, to direct the Foreign Information Service, responsible for foreign broadcasting as well as for the use of other media. By the time of the Japanese attack on Pearl Harbor and the subsequent American entry into the war, Sherwood's group was already making advanced preparations for a broadcasting service.[2]

This service went on the air for the first time on February 24, 1942, in German and directed at Western Europe.[3] The Donovan–Sherwood policy was to restrict themselves to facts. Sherwood rejected using propaganda techniques employed by the Nazis, such as falsehood or terror. The key word in the American effort, he said, would be "Information": "The truth coming from American sincerity is by far the most effective means of propaganda."[4]

This "information" policy was a painful one to follow during the early years of the war, which saw a series of American and British defeats in the Far East and in North Africa. But the credibility of American broadcasts was established, and the policy eventually paid off when the "Voice of America" began to report allied victories.

In June 1942 the Roosevelt administration combined all the information activities of the government into a new organization, the Office of War Information (OWI) under Elmer Davis, a prominent journalist. After some jurisdictional disputes, the control of information for Latin America remained under Nelson Rockefeller as Coordinator of Inter-American Affairs.

Overseas information activities outside Latin America were placed under a branch of the OWI, the U.S. Information Service (USIS). This name has survived all the bureaucratic changes down to the present day and refers to the overseas offices of U.S. information agencies. Robert Sherwood's Foreign Information Service was soon placed under this new organization. Sherwood resigned in 1942 and was succeeded by Edward Barrett, another noted journalist who previously had been an editor of *Newsweek*. The overseas broadcasting efforts of this organization gradually came under the rubric of the "Voice of America," a name that developed as a result of the wording in its early broadcast announcements.

In June 1942 the administration also formed the Office of Strategic Services (OSS), a successor to Colonel Donovan's Office of the Coordinator of Information. The OSS assumed responsibility for foreign intelligence outside of Latin America as well as for psychological warfare operations.

Here again there was some jurisdictional dispute between the OSS's responsibilities for psychological warfare and those of the OWI for information. An uneasy understanding was arrived at under which the OSS restricted itself to "black" propaganda, i.e. information based on clandestine methods and deception, while the OWI concentrated on "open" information based on the optimum utilization of facts.[5]

As the war progressed, the Voice of America arm of the OWI grew until it employed more than 3,000 people and was broadcasting 168 hours a day in over 40 languages. It was estimated that by 1944 about two thirds of the German people were listening to Western broadcasts regularly, either from VOA, the BBC, or French radios.[6] These broadcasts contained not only information and appeals to keep the hopes of liberation alive, but also began to be used as a means of transmitting messages to the undergrounds in these countries.

These "civilian" broadcasts also began to be tied in with a large psychological warfare effort by the allied armed services directed against the Axis military. This effort included armed forces radios and loudspeakers in the field, as well as leaflets and other methods. These operations originated in North Africa and continued on a large scale in Western Europe before and after the Normandy invasion under the direction of Eisenhower's Supreme Headquarters Allied Expeditionary Force (SHAEF). Beyond any doubt, international broadcasting had established itself as an arm of American wartime operations.[7]

1946 — HOLDING OPERATION AND THE
HOPES FOR COEXISTENCE

The approach of peace brought on an almost compulsive back-lash. As Western Europe was gradually liberated from the Nazis in 1944 and victory appeared on the horizon, discussions began in the administration about deactivating U.S. information efforts, including the Voice. In the early memos about possible policies for peacetime, only a few argued for the retention of an American broadcasting capability of some kind. One who did was Nelson Rockefeller, pointing out that radio was "the only medium not subject to foreign censorship or control," the most effective method for getting the American message across to the people of other countries. Elmer Davis and Edward Barrett both recommended the continuation of a reduced Voice operation, but most officials in the State Department and in Congress were unreceptive to the idea. One argument in favor of sustaining a radio organization was a technical one: the transmission facilities and radio band assignments in existence would be difficult to restore later, if it were deemed necessary.[8]

The war officially ended with Japan's formal surrender on September 2, 1945. Throughout the country, in the Truman administration, and in Congress, there was strong sentiment for demobilization and for dismantling of all wartime agencies as rapidly as possible. In addition to the normal desire to "bring the boys home," Americans harbored a native distrust of many aspects of operations like "spying" and "propaganda" in peacetime. In particular, there was little if any sentiment for U.S. information activities in opposition to the U.S.S.R. The overwhelming opinion was that we could and would proceed into the postwar era of peace in a new spirit of cooperation with our former communist allies. Truman quickly abolished the OSS. On August 31, 1945 he also promulgated an executive order terminating the OWI and the propaganda activities of the Office of Inter-American Affairs. Their functions were transferred to an Interim International Information Service, which was supposed to dismantle itself by the end of the year.[9]

Those urging the continuation of some form of broadcasting, such as Davis and Barrett, soon began to be heard in official circles. They were aided by the fact that even before the end of the war, the Soviets were gradually beginning to change the tone of their own broadcasts relating to their allies from generally bland and nondescript to hostile. In Berlin, for example, Radio Berlin had been taken over by the Soviets, and their broadcasts were treating the Western allies more like enemies than friends. Soviet hostility was still only a small, albeit growing, concern in government discussions, but it was enough to provide the margin of success for those advocating some form of continuation of broadcasting on a limited basis.

William Benton, a successful advertising executive and businessman, was appointed Assistant Secretary of State for Public Affairs in September 1945. He was eloquent in advocating the continuation of an information program, including the Voice, before Congress and in the administration. He persuaded Secretary of State Byrnes that a Voice " holding operation" would be the most effective way of reaching people in countries attempting to censor our messages.

Benton cut the staff of the information service and the Voice, but the Congress reduced it even further. By 1946 the number of languages broadcast was down from 41 to 24. The Interim International Information Service went out of service on schedule at the end of 1945, but through the efforts of Benton and others, a permanent Office of International Information and Cultural Affairs (OIC) was set up in the State Department, with an International Broadcasting Division (IBD) to handle the Voice. Benton was able to wrestle a budget of $19.3 million out of Congress for this new organization, of which $7.8 million was for the Voice.[10]

Thus the country emerged into the first postwar year with a skeletal information and broadcasting operation, and with high hopes that even such a limited operation would not be greatly needed in a peaceful world.

NOTES

1. See Thomas C. Sorensen, *The Word War*, (New York: Harper & Row, 1968), pp. 9, 10.

2. See Robert W. Pirsein, *The Voice of America — An History of International Broadcasting Activities of the United States Government 1940–1962*, (New York: Arno Press, 1979), pp. 52–57.
3. Michael A. Hanu, "Not So Long Ago," script for VOA 46th Anniversary Broadcast, February 24, 1982, (Washington, D.C.: USICA), p. 8.
4. Sorensen, pp. 11, 12.
5. Pirsein, pp. 90–92, 95.
6. Sorensen, p. 17.
7. For a discussion of the use of the Voice in psychological warfare, see Sorensen, pp. 12–21; David M. Abshire, *International Broadcasting — A New Dimension of Western Diplomacy*, Washington Papers, Volume IV, No. 35, Center for Strategic and International Studies, Georgetown University, (Beverly Hills: Sage Publications, 1976), pp. 20, 21.
8. Pirsein, pp. 100–102.
9. Pirsein, p. 40; see also pp. 110, 111.
10. Pirsein, p. 112; Leo Bogart, *Premises for Propaganda*, (New York: Free Press, 1976), p. xi.

2

1947-52: Cold War, Hot War, and a Strong Voice

For the next two years Benton mounted an energetic campaign to keep the Voice alive in the face of indifference by Congress, the media, and the public. The mood of the nation, reflected in its foreign policy in early 1946, still assumed that the United States and the Soviet Union would cooperate in maintaining the peace. Spending for propaganda weapons seemed hardly appropriate.

Within a very short time, however, Soviet behavior was eroding that mood of indifference. By the closing months of 1946 and early 1947, it was becoming increasingly clear that the Soviet Union did not share the American vision of postwar collaboration. Soviet authorites installed communist regimes in the liberated territories of Eastern Europe, in violation of the provisions in the Teheran and Yalta Conferences calling for free elections. One blow to Western hopes for peaceful cooperation followed another. As a result of Soviet participation in the war against Japan, the Mongolian Peoples Republic, Inner Mongolia, North Korea, and Sinkiang in China were all brought into the Soviet orbit. In Eastern Europe in 1948, Moscow organized the Communist Information Agency (*Comin-*

11

form), a thinly disguised successor to the Communist International (*Comintern*), which had been suspended as a gesture during World War II. The declared purpose of this organization was to unite the communist states in the forthcoming struggle against "Anglo-American Imperialism."

Communist-instigated revolts erupted in Greece and Turkey. For a growing number in the West, it seemed evident that the U.S.S.R. had not, after all abandoned its erstwhile objective of world revolution. As diplomatic historian Samuel Flagg Bemis wrote "(The Democracies') heritage of freedom, so recently and so valiantly preserved with Russian aid against the Fascist conquest, seemed doomed to another even more formidable trial from their ally of yesteryear."[1] The Truman administration, with James Byrnes, George Marshall, and Dean Acheson serving as successive Secretaries of State, struggled to adjust to this sobering change in American expectations.

One of the earliest responses in Europe was a small but highly significant American broadcasting effort in West Berlin. Literally forced by the flood of hostile propaganda emanating from Soviet-run Radio Berlin, the U.S. occupation authorities took to the air as a cooperative broadcasting venture between the Americans and West Berliners that eventually grew into one of the largest international broadcasting enterprises in Western Europe. This effort was known as RIAS, or Radio in the American Sector, Berlin. RIAS was initiated in February 1946 simply to serve the American sector in Berlin, using telephone lines when the Western Powers were unable to reach agreement with the Soviet representatives on the administration of Berlin Radio. Even this wired service ran into problems with the Soviets since at that time they controlled the postal and telephone services in Berlin. So RIAS took to the airwaves later in 1946, broadcasting in German. Initially the programming was directed only toward the German population in the American Sector, but it later became a major broadcasting service for all of Berlin and East Germany.[2]

RIAS grew beyond anyone's expectations. Those who could hear it in East Germany, Poland, and beyond, responded eagerly. The station received a steady flow of information from listeners and visitors on conditions under communist rule. Beamed back in broadcasts, the effect was huge. Begun as an afterthought, RIAS demonstrated succinctly the power of the word in cold, as well as hot, wars.

When the Soviets began the Berlin blockade in June 1948, the American cooperative broadcasting effort with the Germans, RIAS, assumed much greater political importance. The radio became one of the chief symbols of the Western powers' determination to stay in Berlin and support the West German cause. RIAS broadcasting was expanded greatly and soon covered all zones of Berlin as well as East Germany. Over the next ten years RIAS upgraded its transmission services to include long, medium, shortwave, and FM. Initially funded by the United States, RIAS eventually was staffed almost entirely by Germans, except for a few top executives. It became the first major broadcasting service in history to be operated by citizens of one nationality to broadcast into a country of the same nationality under communist domination. As one German staff member said, it aimed to be "the sort of radio service East Germans would want if they had a choice in the matter."[3] RIAS provided the model of a "surrogate home service" which would prove useful in future broadcasting endeavors.

The management of RIAS developed many of the techniques that were later to become effective with RFE/RL. It built up a large research staff which used interviews with East Germans traveling to the Western zones as well as material from the communist media in East Germany. This staff provided support for the broadcaster so that RIAS was able to furnish East Germans with news and commentaries that were of an immediacy and pertinence not available from their own sources of information.

The service never promoted the idea of an armed uprising, but its commentaries did serve to keep the ideas of democracy alive and to break down the barriers to international communications erected by the communists. The service began a practice that was also to be used effectively by RFE/RL for a time: programming to appeal to "special groups" within the East German population, such as youth, women, farmers, and so on. When the Ulbricht regime began building the Berlin Wall in 1961 and extended the forbidden zone across the entire East German border, RIAS began to assume an even greater responsibility as a "bridge" from the West to East Germany.

RIAS continued to grow in size and importance throughout the 1960s and 1970s. By 1980 the service employed 600 staffers, virtually all West German citizens. Though RIAS continued to operate under the auspices of the United States Information Agency (USIA), the West German government was making financial contributions approximately ten times that of the United States, which in 1980 budgeted only about $1.4 million.[4]

Until recent years, up to around 75 percent of the East German population were estimated to be RIAS listeners. The figure has since dropped to around 40 percent due to competition from West German television. Since most of the transmitters are located around Berlin, and so are surrounded by East Germany, they are difficult to jam.[5]

In March of 1947 Truman announced, and Congress approved, a $400 million program of military and economic aid to Greece and Turkey. The new Truman Doctrine pledged support to any free peoples combatting subversion and armed subjugation by minorities or foreign powers. In June 1947 Secretary of State George Marshall announced the Marshall Plan for the support of the Western European democracies struggling to recover from the war and to resist communist subversion.

These alterations in American public opinion and foreign policy were further expressed in the famous "X" article in *Foreign Affairs* by George Kennan, Director of Policy Planning at the State Department, in July 1947. Entitled "Sources of Soviet Conduct," this article set forth the policy of "containment" against the Soviets. Kennan advocated that strong military barriers be set up to contain the Soviets wherever they threatened further expansion. Containment has often been criticized by those who believe that it is a "no-win" policy, and that the United States needs to formulate a more active program of "rolling back" communism, if only by nonviolent means. But a careful reading of the article shows that Kennan was not simply prescribing passive military containment. In his concluding paragraph Kennan states:

> It is clear that the United States cannot expect in the foreseeable future to enjoy political intimacy with the Soviet regime. It must continue to expect that the Soviet policies will reflect no abstract love of peace and stability, no real faith in the possibility of a permanent happy coexistence . . . but rather a cautious, persistent pressure toward the disruption and weakening of all rival influence and power. This would of itself warrant the United States entering with reasonable confidence upon a policy of firm containment designed to confront the Russians with unalterable counterforce at every point where they show signs of encroaching upon interest of a peaceful and stable world.

This, of course, is the classic definition of containment policy, but Kennan then goes on to say:

> But in actuality the possibilities for American policy are by no means limited to holding the line and hoping for the best. It is entirely possible for the United States to influence by its actions the internal developments, both within Russia and throughout the international Communist movement, by which Russian policy is largely determined. *This is not only a question of the modest measure of informational activity which this government can conduct in the Soviet Union and elsewhere, although that, too, is important.* It is rather a question of the degree to which the United States can create among the peoples of the world generally the impression of a country which knows what it wants, which is coping successfully with the problems of its internal life and with the responsibilities of a World Power, and *which has a spiritual vitality capable of holding its own among the major ideological currents of the time.* To the extent that such an impression can be created and maintained, *the aims of Russian Communism must appear sterile and quixotic, the hopes and enthusiasm of Moscow's supporters must wane, and added strain must be imposed on the Kremlin's foreign policies.*[6] (Emphasis added.)

This significant shift in American foreign policy was reflected on the information and broadcast front. In February 1947 the Voice of America began broadcasting in Russian for the first time. Initially, this effort consisted of only one hour per day of news and features. The program was directed by Charles Thayer, a young Foreign Service Officer with some experience in Russia. Congress, which had been ambivalent on the question of funding for the Voice, now began to show stronger signs of support. In June 1947 the Smith-Mundt Act was introduced in both houses. Passed in January 1948 as Public Law 402, Smith-Mundt gave formal legislative definition for the first time to a U.S. Information Agency, (at that time under State Department auspices and called the Office of International Information and Educational Exchange) and the Voice of America. William Benton resigned soon after as Assistant Secretary of State and was succeeded by George V. Allen. Charles Thayer was named Chief of the Voice.[7]

The Soviets, meanwhile, stepped up the tempo of takeover. In February 1948, with visible Soviet support, a communist faction forcibly seized power in Czechoslovakia, murdering the Czech Foreign Minister, Ian Masaryk. Then in June, the Soviets began a direct assault on the Western powers, blockading Berlin and attempting to take full control of the city. The democracies' recourse was the British-American airlift which kept the city alive for nearly a year until the Soviets, realizing they were losing both the physical and the propaganda battle, called off the blockade in May 1949.

The only favorable development for the West in 1948 was the defection of Yugoslavia under Tito from the Soviet bloc, which took 20 divisions away from Stalin's force assessments. (This event gave some encouragement to the "rollback" school in the American broadcasting fraternity.)

No longer in any doubt about relations with their wartime Soviet ally, the democracies formed the North Atlantic Treaty Organization in April 1949, giving containment a major application. In September the British, French, and Americans allowed the West Germans to form the Federal Republic of Germany, comprising the three western zones of occupation.

Further shocks followed quickly. In the same month of September, the Soviets detonated their first atom bomb, to the consternation of the rest of the world. Mao Zedong's communists completed their conquest of the Chinese mainland, followed shortly by recognition by the U.S.S.R. as the legal government of China. In October the Soviets allowed the East German communists to form the German Democratic Republic, thus formalizing the split of the country that has persisted to the present day.

The escalation of the cold war intensified American interest in broadcasting and international information policy. In a report to the joint Smith-Mundt Congressional Committee on Foreign Relations, the State Department addressed a series of criticisms and suggestions about the U.S. information program, including the VOA, in 1948:

CRITICISM/SUGGESTION: The Congress stated that the VOA must adapt programs to political considerations and needs of a country.

ANSWER: The VOA noted that it had always attempted to tailor its programs to the target area but . . . under the reduced 1948 budget little tailoring was possible. . . . Now, as staffs were enlarged, tailoring was possible.

CRITICISM/SUGGESTION: In order to discomfort local governments and encourage resistance of people in totalitarian and satellite countries, Congress wished that the VOA broadcast news, etc., which such local authorities would seek to suppress.

ANSWER: The VOA commented that it had increased the broadcasting of suppressed news in the countries concerned . . . . Missions are under instructions to furnish whenever possible two such stories daily.[8]

There was growing sentiment that the broadcasting activities must not simply transmit objective news but must be a part of an overall national strategy. George Allen testified before the House Subcommittee on Appropriations in February 1949 and said:

We have entered a new era in foreign relations, infinitely broader than the era of traditional diplomacy. . . . The basic objective of our information program is to assist this Government in the attainment of U.S. national and foreign policy objectives. . . . our operation has been accepted by Congress and is now a permanent and integral part of our foreign relations. . . .[9]

To promote better understanding and cooperation between the information services and the State Department, George Allen brought Foreign Service Officers into the information services for the first time. Allen had been in the Foreign Service himself. This step undoubtedly resulted in better cooperation with State but created institutional controversies which have existed to the present, for instance on the issue of whether Foreign Service Officers are professionally qualified by background for high positions in information and broadcasting work.

The National Security Council produced a detailed study in 1949 which concluded that the United States needed a major information program as well as massive rearmament to counter Soviet aggressiveness. In late 1949 Secretary of State Acheson appointed Edward W. Barrett as Assistant Secretary of State for Public Affairs to replace George Allen. Barrett had built a reputation as a shrewd propagandist in OWI during World War II.

Truman, in a speech to the American Society of Newspaper Editors in April 1950, announced that the United States would launch a major information offensive. Barrett recommended that he call the proposal a "Campaign of Truth" to avoid the connotation of propaganda.

Barrett also outlined four goals for the campaign:

(1) Establish a "healthy international community" with confidence in American leadership.
(2) Present America fairly and counter "all the misrepresentations."
(3) Discourage further Soviet encroachment by showing that America is desirous of peace but is prepared for war.
(4) Help "to roll back Soviet influence" by all means short of force, making the captive peoples feel they can identify with the West, weakening the morale of Soviet officials and military personnel, and "encouraging and strengthening" non-communist forces, including trade unions.[10]

1950 witnessed a sharp and volatile escalation of tension between East and West. On June 25, 1950 a large force of Soviet-made high speed tanks manned by North Korean troops broke across the South Korean border accompanied by an initial force of more than 100,000 troops supplied with Soviet weapons. Meetings of the UN Security Council in succeeding weeks attempted to deal with this new shock to world peace. The Soviets were absent from the Council, having withdrawn earlier in protest against the refusal of the UN to seat Communist China in place of the Nationalists. So without a Soviet veto, the Council was able to declare a breach of the peace and call on all member states to furnish such assistance to the Republic of Korea as might be necessary to repel the attack with a unified command under the United States. Thus the cold war had become a hot war, in which more than 50,000 Americans would lose their lives.

Korea gave added impetus to decisions made during the Berlin crisis, particularly in regard to turning more to the broadcast weapon. The problem was rooted basically in concerns about the future of an Eastern Europe with Soviet-installed client regimes. Many of the leading democratic leaders and cultural figures of these countries had emigrated to the West. Since the United States had extended diplomatic recognition to these regimes, it could not follow the wartime precedent of sponsoring governments-in-exile. But on the other hand, the Truman administration was determined not to accept communist rule as permanent, and to give the exile figures some means of communicating with their fellow citizens behind the Iron Curtain.

General Lucius Clay, who had been Commander of American Forces in Germany in 1948 and 1949, returned to the United States with reports about the success of RIAS in reaching East German audiences. The State Department, including George Kennan and his Policy Planning Staff, devised a plan for a private organization of prominent American citizens to bring together the abilities of prominent East European exiles and assist them in communicating with their homelands. This idea was incorporated as the National Committee for a Free Europe, whose first President was Joseph C. Grew, a retired diplomat. General Clay joined the organization and directed a subsidiary, the Crusade for Freedom, in order to raise money from private sources.

One committee broadcast subsidiary, Radio Free Europe, began transmitting on July 4, 1950. Based in Munich, its broadcasts reached six East European countries: Poland, Czechoslovakia, Romania, Bulgaria, Hungary, and Albania. (Albania was later dropped.)

Since private funding was not considered adequate and the State Department did not want the government to be explicitly identified with the effort, the administration decided to have the CIA provide confidential funds and policy control under State Department guidance.[11] This arrangement remained confidential for many years, and Radio Free Europe thus remained ostensibly a private organization, in contrast to the Voice which was an open and official organ of the U.S. government. In practice, RFE did operate with a greater degree of independence because of the indirect guidance exercised by the U.S. government, as well as by the fact that its mission was to provide a "surrogate home service" rather than a direct reflection of U.S. government policy.

A similar effort directed at the Soviet Union was launched in 1951, called The American Committee for the Freedom of the Peoples of the U.S.S.R. Also ostensibly private, the Committee was in fact financed and controlled by the CIA. Among the Americans providing the initial guidance were such experts on the Soviet Union as Eugene Lyons, Isaac Don Levine, and Francis S. Ronalds, Jr. This Committee also mobilized the abilities of many of the most prominent Russian emigrés. Radio Liberation from Bolshevism went on the air in March 1953 in Russian. Later renamed "Radio Liberty," it augmented its broadcasts over the years to a total of 15 languages, including Russian, Byelorussian, Ukranian, Tatar, Azeri, etc.[12]

Plans for a similar service broadcasting to mainland China known as Radio Free Asia were also initiated in 1951. This service continued to broadcast until 1953 from studios in California, using transmitters in Asia belonging to other countries or organizations. It was disbanded in 1953 during the general budget cutbacks of the new administration and because broadcasts by private church organizations to China had become more active. Some of the broadcasting ideas were developed by various missionary groups broadcasting religious programs and news to North Korea and China from South Korea, Taiwan, and the Philippines. The Far East Broadcasting Company, for example, went on the air in 1951, transmitting from Manila with the mission to carry out "a campaign for freedom based on the teachings and principles of the Lord Jesus Christ."[13]

The missions of Radio Free Europe and Radio Liberation were by definition separate from the Voice, addressing different problems and responsibilities. While the Voice was supposed to be just that, "The Voice of America," reflecting American policy and disseminating world news from an official American viewpoint, the mission of the "private" Radios was to be "surrogate home services." The voices they transmitted to a target country were generally those of emigré nationals of the particular target country, speaking the native language and idiom and reflecting their own interests and concerns.

Problems of mission definition arose on the question of broadcasting objectives. Initially there was strong feeling among many in the Radios for "liberation" and a "rollback" of communism. There was no carefully defined official statement about the form this liberation might take. Many others argued that liberation was unrealizable, and thus deceptive. All maintained that the RFE mission was "to sustain the morale of the *captive* people and stimulate in them a spirit of noncooperation." It was to "remind listeners that they were governed by agents of a foreign power," to demonstrate "the moral and spiritual emptiness of Communism," and to instill "hopes of *eventual* liberation."[14] (Emphasis added.)

Cord Meyer, who assumed responsibility for CIA oversight of RFE/RL in 1954, writes in his memoirs that the State Department had believed that "The promise of democratic freedoms for the Eastern European peoples had been explicit at Yalta and the United States was not prepared to accept as permanent the imposition of Communist rule. . . . It was thought important to keep intact the cadre of democratic leaders who had escaped and to provide them with some way of communicating with their own people in order to keep alive the hope of eventual freedom."[15] Radio Liberation's guidelines spoke of an "implacable struggle against communist dictatorship until its complete destruction."[16]

To carry out these objectives, the two private Radios worked under somewhat different guidelines and organizational plans in the early years when they were still separate entities. Radio Free Europe was broadcasting to six countries with varying cultures and traditions and long histories of antagonisms among themselves. But all had been close to Western European civilization and culture, and regarded themselves as ruled by a regime imposed by a foreign power. Even within each of the emigré communities there were factional antagonisms. There was also a high degree of emotionalism, in that most of the emigrés had relatives, friends, or associates who had been imprisoned, tortured, or killed by the communists. They had seen their countries brutally taken over. Most had to flee for their lives. Many had lost substantial property. It was natural they would approach the possibilities of broadcasting back to their countries with some emotion, and with hopes for eventual liberation.

Cord Meyer said that the Americans in charge of programming soon learned that they could not simply turn the microphones over to the emigrés and let them start broadcasting. The organizational structure that evolved at RFE had Americans in charge of the broadcasting, who would appoint the emigrés as chiefs of the five country desks. In cooperation with these desk chiefs, the scriptwriters and broadcasters were then hired on the basis of talent and ability.

> Policy control over content was obtained by the formulation of general guidelines, supplemented by daily meetings with the American policy advisers to determine the handling of specific news items. Out of this compromise arrangement emerged the fruitful partnership between exile talent and American policy advisers that has made RFE broadcasts so widely popular and so well respected to this day. . . .[17]

A Central News Desk was established at RFE, which over the years came to be staffed by professional journalists, mainly Americans (and later British Commonwealth citizens). This desk received dispatches from the leading international news services, AP, UPI, Reuters, Agence France Presse, etc., as well as from TASS and other communist services, and eventually from RFE's own correspondents in leading capitals. From this collection the Central Desk compiled an hourly set of releases, which was distributed to the country desks. The country desks were given guidelines on how to handle the news releases at a morning meeting and by guidance memos from the Policy Advisor. Each country desk was then responsible for translating the material to be broadcast and putting it on the air in the language of the country. The country desk was allowed some flexibility in originating material of interest to the particular country, and in deciding which of the Central News Desk items to broadcast, but the scripts were ultimately reviewed by a special unit to ensure adherence to internal policy guidelines.

This organizational scheme at RFE is still functioning. Its practical and operational precepts have varied as RFE policy reflected the changes in American foreign policy. Controversies and tensions have arisen between American management and the emigré staff of the country desks, and even within the staffs of each desk, for instance between those favoring a stronger or milder line against communism. These differences have in their own way reflected the controversies within the general U.S. public.

Radio Liberation was organized on a different basis at the beginning. The founders realized that they faced a more difficult problem. As Sergei Sabur says in *Kontinent*,

> However, "Radio Liberation," later renamed "Radio Liberty," had nothing in common with 'Radio Free Europe' in the character of its transmissions. From the beginning its founders understood one thing: they were faced with the task of conducting a conversation not with Europeans who had lost their independence only a few years before, but with the population of an isolated, stricken country, the people of which had been subjected to persecution for three decades and more, and were still experiencing the most nightmarish terror in the history of nations — in addition to the natural difficulties of the post-war period.[18]

Radio Liberation thus faced the formidable task of countering the propaganda that the Russian people had been subjected to for over 30 years. While the Soviet information organs had moderated their propaganda against the West during the World War II alliance, the familiar rhetoric was reinstated with full force and virulence soon after the peace, replete with the old slogans of "imperialism," "capitalist encirclement," and so forth. While these themes were used in Moscow's global propaganda campaign, they also became basic elements in internal propaganda, which Radio Libertation felt an obligation to counter.

It was assumed that the Soviet people had been so conditioned by this propaganda that normal news or commentaries from Western radios would have little or no effect on them, and conceivably could be counterproductive. For example, news about American political campaigns, which American commentators might think would impress the Soviet people with democratic institutions, was often in fact almost incomprehensible. A typical reaction might be, "What difference does it make which party is in power in a capitalist country?" Most Russians are educated to believe that the masses in America are pro-communist, the unemployed are starving, and the capitalists manipulate the political process protected by the police. Likewise, news about government crises in France or Italy would be met with similar indifference. "What was the importance of changes in the bourgeois parties in these capitalist countries?" News about the Marshall Plan was dismissed by many in the East with the reaction that it was simply an American scheme for buying Western European support with a can of spam. Strong anti-Soviet statements broadcast by VOA might be dismissed as simply outbursts "by former White Guards or Hitlerites who would do anything for money." Descriptions of day-to-day living by Americans with details on their comfortable material life were unbelievable lies "too good to be true."[19]

To try to overcome these obstacles, the Russian emigrés were given more scope than in RFE. More of the editors were Russians, and they were allowed more creative freedom in their programming. An American political coordinator had the right to censor programs, but there are no reports of this right being exercised.

The news divisions at RL also worked differently from those at RFE. The news editors received dispatches from the same array of news services but selected only those items considered to be of interest to the people of the U.S.S.R. The dispatches were sent to the writers section for translation into Russian but the writers were free to add detailed explanations, going far beyond the original text if necessary. For this work they could call upon the resources of a Research Department, which was built up over the years into a large organization, making its resources available to outside scholars. This department amassed a library of 50,000 books on Russia and newspaper files going back to the early days of the Revolution. Such files provided an exceptional resource base for a radio service broadcasting back into the U.S.S.R. The library also contained biographical material and historical reference works, enabling the newswriters to build up a framework for the news and to compare releases from the Western news services with TASS. These facilities were aimed at creating a broadcasting network closely attuned to its Soviet listenership.[20]

Such writing required more time than the quick editing of dispatches which was the norm at RFE. Radio Liberation, however, did not feel the kind of pressures competing with the ponderous Soviet news services that were experienced at RFE, which had to vie with the Eastern European services.

Some RFE personnel who perhaps did not appreciate this difference joked that Radio Liberation did not have a "newsroom" at all, only a type of "weekly magazine" organization.[21] But the Radio Liberation people were convinced that they faced a different kind of competition for timeliness, and they worked out a method that would have the maximum impact on their listeners.

Like RFE, Radio Liberation made use of the abilities of a great number of able emigrés for commentaries and discussions. These included experts in history, the arts, and religion. RL had the services of Father Alexandr Schmemann of St. Vladimir's Theological School in Tuckahoe, N.Y., a Russian Orthodox priest who broadcast a regular series of sermons and lectures. Solzhenitsyn listened regularly while in the Soviet Union and called him "my favorite preacher." When Solzhenitsyn arrived in the United States after his expulsion from Russia, Father Schmemann was the first man he asked to speak with.[22]

Readings of underground literature became an important feature. A great volume of illegal writing has grown up within the Soviet Union, novels, essays, poetry, political commentary, etc. that is typed, mimeographed, or printed on crude home presses and passed from hand to hand. This is known as *samizdat.* A certain amount finds its way abroad and is published there, known as *tamizdat.* By broadcasting selected readings of this literature, Radio Liberation was able to increase its coverage tremendously within the U.S.S.R. (The Radio Liberty library still maintains an archive of this literature.)

Radio Liberation had its own correspondents in New York, Washington, Paris, London, Rome and occasionally sent reporters on special assignment to other cities. These correspondents would broadcast news and commentary from the respective cities, highlighting material that would be of interest to listeners in the Soviet Union.

Both "Freedom Radios," thus, were in the thick of the Cold War from the moment of their births. They were considered key elements in a broad counteroffensive that brought together all available resources under a top level Psychological Strategy Board (PSB). The PSB's job was to see that all activities with information and psychological impact were coordinated for optimum effect.

An immediate consequence of this new offensive was an upgrading of the Voice of America. In July 1950 the U.S. Advisory Commission on Information said in its report to the President and Congress:

> The propaganda effort of the USSR, now bordering on open psychological warfare, is a major threat to this Government's foreign policy objectives . . . a psychological offensive by the United States based on truth is essential if the United States is to succeed in its foreign policy objectives . . . .[23]

In this climate, the budgets of the Voice were increased appreciably. While William Benton had to fight to keep the Voice barely alive in 1946, George Allen succeeded in getting a budget through Congress of $6.9 million for 1949. Even that was low compared with just a short time later. By fiscal 1951 Edward Barrett was able to have this figure almost doubled, to $13.1 million.

Foy Kohler was brought in as VOA Director in October 1949. A Foreign Service Officer with almost 20 years experience, most recently as Chargé d'Affairs in Moscow, he had a reputation as one of the country's leading experts on the Soviet Union. He later served as Ambassador to Moscow, and subsequently as Assistant Secretary of State for European Affairs.[24]

The Voice's tone and program content became much sharper, with outspoken commentaries, attacks on personalities, and anti-communist political analyses. Two examples:

When is a germ not a germ? When is an epidemic not an epidemic? Who is sick and who is not sick? These are the problems facing the Communist world today. . . . on April 8 the representative for the Korean People's Democratic Republic— that's the Communist gobbledygook for Communist North Korea—rose to his feet to address the International Economic Conference—and that's Communist gobbledygook for a circus going on in Moscow right now the correct title of which is "Who'll do business with Stalin? Butter will melt in his mouth."

VOA Commentary, 1951: *Germ Warfare.*

Just recently, Czechoslovakia Minister of Health, Josef Plojhar, addressing a so-called peace meeting in Prague, praised Stalin as "our great Christian leader." To be more explicit, he said, and I quote: "The people of East Europe now form a new Christian world under the leadership of the great Josef Vissarionovich Stalin. . . ."

Now, if you are surprised that the atheist Josef Stalin should suddenly be elevated to the office of leader of the Christian world you must be doubly surprised that such an elevation should take place through the mouth of a Minister of Health. After all the generalissimo has his own suborned clergy right here in Moscow. If he had desired, and obviously his silence denotes his desire, he could have had one of these elevate him to the place of leader of the Christian world.

VOA Commentary, 1951: *Stalin, the New Apostle.*[25]

At the end of 1950, Director Kohler summarized the objectives of the VOA in an address before the Speech Association of America:

> The attempt of Soviet propaganda to convince the world that the United States is a warmongering, power-hungry nation, determined to dominate all other nations, has reached a point where it can only be described as aggressive psychological warfare and a major threat to the foreign policy objectives of the U.S. . . . This situation points up the vital need for reaching the Russian people with the true story of American aims and purposes. . . . the role of the Voice of America in this effort is an important one because of the ability of radio to surmount the man-made barriers of censorship and suppression, and speak directly to the people.
>
> . . . . Under the present expansion program, the broadcast output will be practically doubled. . . . Propaganda must be made a potent weapon in our effort to avoid another great conflict. . . .[26]

In March 1951 Kohler testified before the House Appropriations Subcommittee on the broadcasting practices of the Voice:

> . . . we remind them (the people of Eastern Europe) of their own glorious traditions. We remind them of their own history. We remind them of their own literature, in cases where they have been suppressed by the Soviet regime . . . we speak our mind about the Soviet regime without much hesitation. At the same time we have not adopted the violent and vicious language of our opponent, in that sense. We are a little more dignified as well as a little more convincing, I trust. . . . we try to take a very positive line but without engaging in any direct exchange of polemic with them, because one of the first rules of propaganda is that you do not let your adversary call the tune. . . .[27]

As noted above, Kohler's remarks against polemics were not always followed by his writers. Under his direction, in fact, the Voice continued to take a strikingly activist tone against communism. It also gained a new peak of support by the Administration and Congress. The budget for fiscal year 1953 was $21.7 million, almost triple the budget of four years earlier, and a level that was not to be reached again for ten years.

As new Program Manager of the Voice, Barry Zorthian and his assistants prepared a handbook for the news staff in the closing days of 1952. The book was not actually issued until February 1953, a few days after Eisenhower's inauguration. But it represents the thinking of Voice management on program policy in the closing days of the Truman administration. There was to be some reduction in staff under Eisenhower and some change in emphasis, but the broad outlines of policy would remain highly similar. The following is the introduction to the handbook:

OBJECTIVES

The general mission of the United States Government's international information program may be broken down into five specific objectives:

(1) to multiply and intensify psychological deterrents to Communist aggression;

(2) to stimulate confidence in the Government and the People of the United States among peoples of the Free World, particularly in Western Europe;

(3) to combat neutralism, particularly in Asia and the Middle East;

(4) to maintain hope of ultimate liberation and identification with the free world among peoples behind the Iron Curtain;

(5) to encourage recognition of mutuality of interest on the part of peoples traditionally linked with the United States, particularly in Latin America.

These are fairly general concepts. How do they apply to a day-to-day news operation? As a matter of practice, these concepts are translated into specific guidances for handling the day's news developments—known as policy. More on policy later. But these general objectives do outline the only reason for our existence. They should make clear to you that we are not in business to amuse, entertain or simply inform our listeners. Nor are we in business because news is an end in itself. The United States is in the midst of a serious struggle for the mind of mankind and the only purpose of the News Branch — as well as the entire Voice of America—is to contribute toward winning that struggle.

So let there be no doubt that as participants in this effort, we are a propaganda agency in the best sense of the word and an instrument of United States foreign policy.

Under "News Treatment" the manual goes on to say:

Accuracy as to the facts you use is perhaps the most important standard you have. You can interpret them and point them up by selection, organization, and emphasis, but don't try to change them. . . . Again your tool is skillful writing. And again the basic validity of your position is all the more reason you can afford to be accurate in yours facts.

Let the enemy propagandist resort to the name-calling and shouting. They have a great deal to hide. You can adopt a calmer and more sober tone. In the long run it is a much better way to keep friends and influence people because it breeds confidence in you. But don't confuse restraint with dullness. Slogans, catchy phrases, simple thoughts, clear cut objectives are all necessary and are not incompatible with restraint . . . .

Our approach should be one of positive propaganda. We are "for" things, not only "against" them. Keep your output as positive as possible and avoid being dragged into arguments with the opposing propagandists. . . . You should seek to give your listener an ideal and a way of life to support rather than a system merely to oppose.[28]

NOTES

1. S. F. Bemis, *A Diplomatic History of the United States*, (New York: Holt, Rinehart and Winston, 1965), p. 927.
2. Donald R. Browne, *International Radio Broadcasting*, (New York: Praeger Publishers, 1982), pp. 132, 133.
3. Browne, p. 133.

4. Ibid., pp. 133–135.
5. Abshire, p. 28.
6. *Foreign Affairs*, July 1947, pp. 566–582.
7. Pirsein, pp. 127–144.
8. "U.S. Information Service in Europe, Implementation by the Department of State of the Recommendations Contained in the Reports of the Committee on Foreign Relations (Smith-Mundt Congressional Group), January 1948–February 1949," pp. 10, 11.
9. Department of State Appropriations Bill for 1950, Hearings, House, pp. 716–718.
10. Edward W. Barrett, *Truth is our Weapon* (New York: Funk & Wagnalls, 1953) pp. 78, 79.
11. Cord Meyer, *Facing Reality — From World Federalism to the CIA*, (New York: Harper & Row, 1980), p. 111.
12. Sabur, pp. 3–4.
13. Donald R. Browne, "International Broadcasting to Asia" in *Broadcasting in Asia and the Pacific*, (Philadelphia: Temple University Press, 1978) edited by John A. Lent, p. 318.
14. Library of Congress, Congressional Research Service, 1972, "Radio Free Europe — A Survey and Analysis," quoted in Abshire, p. 31.
15. Meyer, p. 111.
16. Library of Congress, 1972, "Radio Liberty—A Study of Its Origins, Structure, Policy, Programming, and Effectiveness," quoted in Abshire, p. 31.
17. Meyer, p. 112.
18. Sabur, p. 3.
19. Sabur, pp. 1, 2.
20. Sabur, p. 4.
21. Interviews with former RFE language desk writers and editors.
22. Sabur, p. 5.
23. U.S. Advisory Commission on Information, "Third Report to the President and Chairman of the State and House Committees," July 14, 1950, p. 1.
24. Pirsein, pp. 200, 201.
25. Quoted in Pirsein, pp. 198, 199.
26. Ibid., p. 207.
27. Ibid., p. 209.
28. "This Is Your Job," internal VOA publication by Barry Zorthian and Harold Berman, News Branch, International Broadcasting Division, February 1, 1953.

3
1953–60: Retrenchment and Revision
of Mission

Aggressive as the Zorthian guidelines were, they were not vigorous enough for the opposition. During the Eisenhower presidential campaign, the Voice was attacked for not taking a
strong enough line. Secretary of State-to-be John Foster Dulles
was calling for a more active policy of liberation and attacked
the Truman administration for its "no-win" policy of containment. Senator Joseph McCarthy (R–Wis.) was also gearing up
his campaign of accusations about communist infiltration, and
one of his primary targets was the information offices of the
State Department.

After Eisenhower's inauguration in January 1953, the new
administration, the first Republican regime in twenty years,
launched a series of investigations into government information operations. During 1953, there were no fewer than six
such studies done by committees of the executive branch or
Congress which examined the Voice of America. These included the President's Committee on International Information Activities under William Jackson, the President's Advisory
Committee on Government Reorganization under Nelson
Rockfeller, a special Committee in the State Department's In-

ternational Information Agency to evaluate U.S. information activities, and the annual survey by the U.S. Advisory Commission on Information. The Senate launched a study by the Senate Committee on Foreign Relations under Senator Bourke Hickenlooper (R–Iowa) at the same time that Joseph McCarthy took over the chairmanship of the Subcommittee on Investigations of the Senate Committee on Government Operations and began to probe into American information activities.

The State Department's information activities came under sharp criticism from several of these bodies for being overblown, inefficient, and lacking direction and focus. McCarthy also launched a major campaign to show that they were riddled with subversives.

Before these investigations went very far, events in Europe intervened in a shattering way. Stalin died in March 1953. After an initial period of obscure maneuvering behind the Kremlin walls, his successors launched a new "peace offensive." Rumor had it, for example, that they were considering moves toward peaceful German reunification. Whatever the truth behind the rumors, the new Soviet leadership aroused considerable hopes for peaceful coexistence with the West. Eisenhower replied with a major speech on peace in April, offering steps towards disarmament and a fund for world aid and reconstruction in a worldwide war on poverty.

Then, on June 17, 1953 there was an uprising of workers in East Berlin and several hundred other East German towns and cities, in protest over communist labor policies. USIA, the Voice, and both Radios initially made full use of the events in communications to the communist countries and the rest of the world. USIA disseminated many photographs of angry young Germans throwing rocks at Soviet tanks in East Berlin and published stories of unarmed rioters being gunned down by Soviet machine guns and tanks. But when the question of actual support of the rebels was faced, the United States decided it could not, and should not, do anything to aid the uprising. Those officials in the Radios, the administration, and especially in the information agencies who had been advocating a liberation policy were deeply disappointed. The East Berlin event was the first practical demonstration of the fact that the United States could not always back up with military action its inclination to assist those resisting communist domination. "Liberation" was not to be the policy goal, except as a vague hope for the future. From here on, the Radios were especially careful not to call for or advocate open rebellion.

The result of these traumatic experiences and the many surveys was a major reorganization of American information activities, which in turn meant a serious reduction in the operations of the Voice. The VOA budget for fiscal 1954 was 36 percent less than the 1953 budget. There were to be no major additions to Voice transmission facilities for the next four years.

It seemed to many ironic that the Eisenhower administration, after campaigning on a platform that advocated more energetic policies to counter communist propaganda, was now reducing the size of the international information effort. But this was a period of wholesale reductions in force throughout the Federal bureaucracy, and the Voice was a prime target for those looking to reduce government "waste."

Some organizational changes, however, were considered valuable by all concerned and have remained in force. All information activities were transferred from the State Department to an independent body for the first time: the United States Information Agency (USIA). This agency reported directly to the President, with the National Security Council in an advisory role, though the State Department retained some authority to guide "policy." The Voice of America was reorganized as a department of USIA.

John Foster Dulles, although a believer in a strong anticommunist policy, was less interested in propaganda than many other Secretaries of State. He did not take very seriously the role of public opinion abroad, convinced that the United States should pursue the "right" foreign policy and that public opinion would follow along. He was more concerned with diplomacy and launched a major effort to promote collective security with a system of alliances around the periphery of the communist world, resulting in the Baghdad Pact and the SEATO. Thus, he did not resist having American information activities moved out from under the State Department.[1]

Eisenhower was a firm believer in propaganda after his experiences in World War II, but he did not give the U.S. information program the active support that it was to receive later from John F. Kennedy. The name of the Psychological Strategy Board was changed to the Operations Coordinating Board. Thus under Eisenhower and Dulles, too, the budgets for the entire information program remained low. But there was a continuation of the anti-communist tone and more emphasis on efficiency and clearer objectives, consistant with the new administration's stress on fiscal retrenchment.

The Voice also moderated its programming tone considerably. The Jackson Committee, although it included several men who were enthusiastic propagandists such as C. D. Jackson (no relation to the chairman), a former *TIME Inc.* Vice President who presided over the new National Committee for a Free Europe, John Hughes, also of the National Committee, and Sigurd Larson, President of Young and Rubicam, issued a report that recommended a more calm and persuasive tone. The idea of liberation was still present but in a far less urgent manner. "The primary and overriding purpose of the information program," said the report, "should be to submit evidence to the peoples of other nations that their own aspirations for freedom, progress, and peace are supported and advanced by the objectives and policies of the United States."[2]

Across the world, developments in Asia added to the changes. In July 1953, after some determined behind-the-scenes diplomacy by the administration, the North Koreans signed a truce at Panmunjom agreeing to an armistice. This agreement remained tenuous and was prone to violations for years, but it did contribute to an amelioration of tensions. These events served to make the Voice's programming somewhat more muted, while at the same time its personnel was being reduced.

Theodore Streibert was appointed as the head of the new USIA in 1953. He was a broadcasting executive from the private sector, having served as President of the Mutual Broadcasting System and station WOR. Henry Loomis, whom Streibert brought in as his assistant and who later became Director of the Voice, later said that Streibert was exactly the sort of hard-driving executive that USIA needed at the time. "His feeling was that the whole operation was a bowlfull of jelly. Streibert was a manager, rather than a leader. He established the framework the Agency is still using today. . . . In short, he made the machine. Directors after him worried about how to use the machine."[3]

On October 22, 1953, Eisenhower issued a Statement of Mission for the USIA that served as an important guide to policy for several years. The document read in part:

> The purpose of the United States Information Agency shall be to submit evidence to the peoples of other nations by means of communication techniques that the objectives and policies of the United States are in harmony with and will advance their legitimate aspirations for freedom, progress, and peace.[4]

Under Streibert, the Voice concentrated its efforts on broadcasts to the communist countries. About 75 percent of its transmission were directed to countries behind the Iron or Bamboo Curtains by 1954. Many other language services were eliminated and not restored for several years.

 Although budgets were lower than in previous years, Streibert reported that morale had recovered after the initial personnel cuts, and that broadcasting to communist areas was more effective and concentrated. The idea of "liberation" or the "rollback" of communism had been discredited to a major extent, but concepts of encouraging nonviolent change in the communist regimes still lingered in discussions about objectives. For example, on December 1, 1954, Streibert spoke at a dedication ceremony for the new Washington studios. He said in part:

> One of the principal objectives of the Voice is to bring the truth about the policies of the United States . . . to the peoples of the Soviet Orbit by penetrating through the Iron and Bamboo Curtains. . . .
>
> To the enslaved peoples of the Satellites our news and commen-

taries from the outside world can also continue to bring evidence of our *interest in their freedom and hope for their ultimate liberation.*[5] (Emphasis added.)

Meanwhile, Radio Free Europe and Radio Liberation were augmenting their operations. Broadcasts to Iron Curtain countries would gradually supplant much of the work that VOA had done in reaching the people in communist countries with local news. Thus, as time went on this particular aspect of VOA broadcasting could be scaled down so more VOA funds could be devoted to broadcasting to other parts of the world.

The budget for Radio Free Europe was not cut as much as that of the Voice during this period, declining only 16 percent during the first year of the Eisenhower administration compared to 36 percent for the Voice. Radio Liberation's budget actually increased slightly during the period since it was still in its formative stages. (See a summary of yearly budgets in Appendix I.)

Both organizations were expanding their research organizations and libraries. In addition to furnishing valuable back-up materials to the radio writers and editors, research facilities also became important sources of information on communist countries, and their published reports and libraries were made available to media representatives as well as to scholars.

This was the period that Nikita Khrushchev attained the dominant position in the Soviet leadership. Khrushchev preached "goulash communism" and reform of the harsher features of Stalin's rule. For the first time since the war, detente of a sort took hold between the superpowers. In 1955, leaders of East and West met at the summit in Geneva. Forceful psychological offensives were not the order of the day.

Not for long. By 1956 tension was increasing in Eastern Europe, and it turned out to be a major year of crisis for RFE. In February, Khrushchev made his famous speech at the 20th Communist Party Congress in which he denounced Stalin. This speech was obtained by the CIA and made available to the American media. Both Radios broadcast the oration in detail to the communist countries. One result of the speech, amplified by its greater dissemination by RFE and RL, was to increase opposition both inside and outside the communist parties of Eastern Europe to Stalinist repression. In Poland, Boleslaw Bierut, the leader most closely associated with Stalin, died in March, and the deputy premier, Jakob Berman, was forced to resign in May.

A more moderate leader, Wladyslaw Gomulka, was released from prison. In June a workers' revolt broke out in Poznan to protest a reduction in wages. This uprising was immediately quelled by the Polish security forces, resulting in 53 killed and several hundred wounded. Demands increased for the return of Gomulka to power, and in October the Central Committee elected him Premier. The Russian Marshal, Rokossovsky, was relieved as head of the Polish Armed Forces. Khrushchev flew to Warsaw with other Soviet leaders in October. In a confrontation with the new Polish leaders, and facing possible resistance by armed Polish workers, they backed down and allowed the Poles to maintain some degree of autonomy.[6]

Throughout this period, RFE broadcast factual details as much as possible but was careful to advise restraint and to avoid any implication that the Poles could succeed in an armed uprising against their communist rulers and the Soviets. But that did not spare RFE from accusations that it had instigated or at least encouraged the uprising.

Similar events were taking place in Hungary during 1956, though on a much wider scale. Encouraged by Soviet compromises in Poland, Hungarian workers, students, and intellectuals began to agitate for similar concessions. As a result of both clumsy maneuvering by the Hungarian government and bold actions by the Hungarian people, a full-scale revolt broke out. Crowds toppled Stalin's statue in Budapest, workers seized arms from the factories, and most of the Hungarian Army and the regular police joined the revolt throughout the country. All of the provincial radios were seized. The hated security police were defeated, with many fatalities. The leaders of the revolt demanded abolition of the one party system and the security police, restoration of parlimentary democracy, withdrawal of Soviet troops, and a proclamation of Hungarian neutrality. After some duplicitous hints at accommodation, Soviet tanks rolled into Budapest.

The Hungarian communist top men fled the country. A more moderate Party leader, Imre Nagy, announced a coalition government and proclaimed a ceasefire, promising free elections, and proclaiming Hungarian neutrality. The Soviets stalled for time, bringing further troops into the country. On November 4, Janos Kadar, Secretary of the Hungarian Communist Party under Nagy, betrayed his boss, announced a new cabinet, and appealed to the Soviets for troops to put down the "forces of Fascism and reaction." Nagy was captured through a ruse and later executed in Russia. The Soviet Army then crushed the rebellion, with fighting continuing for more than six weeks.[7]

RFE's role in the rebellion remains controversial. It was accused by the Soviets, the Kadar government, and some critics in the United States and West Europe, of having instigated a hopeless revolt against the Hungarian government.

Cord Meyer, who was in charge of CIA oversight of the Radios at that time, says that on the contrary, the CIA and RFE were caught by surprise by the armed uprising and did not have any prepared policy for reporting it. The general policy was to report the facts, without issuing any signals indicating that the revolt would be supported by American armed intervention. Eisenhower, it should be noted, had made that most clear to Khrushchev immediately after the uprising started.

The transmission of hard and prompt news by RFE of the progress of the revolt undoubtedly did something to prolong it, when a complete news blackout, such as the communists tried to impose, might have hastened its defeat. Later there were careful investigations, not only by American authorities in the CIA and the State Department, but also by the West German Government and the Council of Europe, which felt some responsibility since the RFE broadcasts originated from German soil. These probes included careful reviews of RFE broadcast tapes during the crisis. All studies agreed that RFE had not inspired the revolt nor given it undue encouragement. Cord Meyer believes that the only fault found with the broadcasts was perhaps in tone: too much enthusiasm and optimism, and too little regard for the unlikelihood of any effective support from the UN or the Western powers.[8]

The crushing of this Hungarian revolt, which resulted in the death of hundreds of the finest young "freedom fighters" in Hungary, was another blow to those in the Radios and the U.S. administration still backing a policy of liberation. Meyer says that the American management of RFE made several "personnel changes" in the leadership of the Hungarian desk. A number of the most talented new emigrés, who presumably had a more realistic idea of what could be accomplished through broadcasting were brought on staff after the revolt.

As a result of the Hungarian experience, from 1957 onwards the American broadcasts were even more severely restricted in content although they continued to be guided by the idea that the Soviets represented a threat to world peace and the interests of the democracies. Liberation became in effect a hope for liberalization, evolution rather than revolution.

The main objective of the broadcast policies of RFE/RL after 1956 can be summarized under two headings: (1), to provide complete, prompt, accurate news, both of the world as well as news of the respective countries that may have been censored by the communist authorities, and (2), to express and relate the ideas and concepts of Western society. The latter theme was done with the idea that only the peoples of these countries could manage liberation through their own efforts, working within their own societies to encourage perhaps gradual breakdowns of the tyrannies under which they lived. But this could only be hoped for if the ideas of Western democracy were kept alive in these countries. Thus the outcome was an uneasy compromise in broadcast policy, reflecting broader foreign policy itself.

Continuing efforts by the Soviets to promote "peaceful coexistence" had some effect in mitigating the rhetoric of American radio broadcasts. U.S.-Soviet cultural agreements were renewed. In the summer of 1959 the United States was permitted to stage a National Exhibition in Moscow for the first time, with a similar exhibition mounted by the Soviets in New York City. USIA set up what it called "ten acres of America in the heart of Moscow for six weeks." In one model home at the exhibit, Vice President Richard Nixon had his famous "kitchen debate" with Khrushchev.

Khrushchev visited the United States later in 1959, and the Soviets soon ceased their jamming of the Voice of America. Eisenhower, Khrushchev and their advisers held discussions at Camp David. American "provocative" broadcasting to Eastern Europe was one topic raised by the Soviets, after which the Americans raised the issue of jamming. Despite lack of agreement on this issue, the Soviets did reduce jamming for several months. Party propaganda organs made much of the "Spirit of Camp David," though it was soon apparent that Khrushchev was actively pursuing a foreign policy of aggressive support for communist expansion abroad, as for example, sponsoring the communist Pathet Lao rebellion in Laos.[9]

Although efforts at greater Soviet-American understanding resulted in moderating the sharp tone of U.S. broadcasts and the support for liberation, programming policies did continue to promote the concept of ultimate progress towards more liberty through the efforts of the people themselves in the Soviet bloc. Some indication of this sentiment in Washington was provided by the Captive Nations Week Resolution, passed by the Congress and signed by the President on July 17, 1959. The passage of this bill indicated that a majority in Congress continued to regard the communists as a threat to world peace and liberty, and it confimed official American advocacy of peaceful progress towards freedom in the communist countries. The declaration spoke of "the enslavement of a substantial part of the world's population by Communist imperialism" and the "aggressive policies of Russian Communism (which) poses a dire threat to the security of the United States and of all the free peoples. . . ." It states that the "submerged nations look to the United States as the citadel of human freedom, for leadership in bringing about their liberation."

The resolution added that "the desire for liberty and independence by the overwhelming majority of the people of these submerged nations constitutes a powerful deterrent to war and one of the best hopes for a just and lasting peace. . . ." Accordingly, the President was to issue an annual proclamation designating the third week in July as "Captive Nations Week," and to issue a similar proclamation each year until "such time as freedom and independence shall have been achieved for all the captive nations of the world."[10]

Eisenhower issued such a proclamation. In future years the wording of this proclamation by each President would be an important barometer of the feelings in his administration regarding the importance of the communist threat to liberties, as well as the desire to avoid offending the Soviets and thus jeopardize arms and trade negotiations.[11]

The concluding years of the Eisenhower administration also set the stage for a protracted struggle over policy between two groups within the Voice, USIA, and the State Department over Voice policy. The two faction can be described roughly as the "objectivity" school and the "mission" school. Thomas C. Sorensen, who became second in command at USIA under Edward R. Murrow in 1961, says in his book, *The Word War*, that he believes Voice officials pushed the pendulum too hard in the direction of "objectivity" by 1959. Too much VOA broadcasting, he says, became merely pointless. There were several disputes between the policy desks and the broadcasters. Eisenhower became involved in one incident, which he recounted in his autobiography:

> I had been told that a representative of the Voice of America had tried to obtain from a Senator a statement opposing our landing of troops in Lebanon. In a state of some pique I informed Secretary Dulles that this was carrying the policy of "free broadcasting" too far. The Voice of America should, I said, employ truth as a weapon in support of free world objectives, but it had no mandate or license to seek evidence of lack of domestic support of America's foreign policy and actions.[12]

By 1959 the Director of the Voice, Henry Loomis, decided that the organization needed a statement of principles, "a formal base from which we could fight our battles as a strategic instrument." Over the next year a charter was drawn up, a cooperative effort of many key staff members including Loomis, Zorthian, and later George V. Allen. The final document issued in 1960 read as follows:

The VOA Charter:
The long-range interests of the United States are served by communicating directly with the peoples of the world by radio. To be effective, the Voice of America must win the attention and respect of listeners. These principles will govern VOA broadcasts:

1. VOA will establish itself as a consistently reliable and authoritative source of news. VOA news will be accurate, objective, and comprehensive.
2. VOA will represent America, not any single segment of American society. It will therefore present a balanced and comprehensive projection of significant American thought and institutions.
3. As an official radio, VOA will present the policies of the United States clearly and effectively. VOA will also present responsible discussion and opinion on these policies.[13]

This statement can, in fact, be interpreted to support the policies of either the "objectivity" or "mission" schools of thought. It became the governing document within the Voice from then on, and for many years it was used to justify a strong broadcasting policy of countering communist ideology.

In 1976, however, the VOA Charter was introduced in Congress by Senator Charles Percy (R–Ill.) and Representative Bella Abzug (D–N.Y.) as part of Public Law 94-350, signed by President Gerald Ford. It became the principal legal authority cited by those in the Voice arguing for a policy of "objectivity." Yet it should be noted that the Charter was initially promulgated by officials who believed the Voice should be used as one of the "strategic instruments" of U.S. foreign policy.

In 1960, Voice executives wanted to have the charter promulgated by the National Security Council, in order to give it more clout. Eisenhower demurred, arguing that he had provided the USIA with a Statement of Mission. Sorensen, who assumed his position at USIA the following year, says in his 1968 book that, viewed with hindsight, the Charter "does not go far enough, and is ambiguous and vague."[14]

Thus the lines were being drawn between the "objectivity" and "mission" factions in the broadcasting organizations. In practice, the VOA Charter was not frequently referred to publicly until it was brought out by those seeking to ehance the "objectivity" of Voice broadcasts in the late 1970s. But this trend developed under entirely unforeseen circumstances, and the Voice operated for some years as the "strategic instrument" envisioned by those such as Henry Loomis and George Allen.

NOTES

1. Sorensen, pp. 53, 54.
2. Quoted in Pirsein, p. 320.
3. Ibid., p. 329.
4. Quoted in Sorenson, p. 49.
5. Quoted in Pirsein, p. 344.
6. Meyer, pp. 120, 121.
7. Ibid., pp. 123–125.
8. For a discussion of RFE Policy during the Hungarian uprising, see Meyer, pp. 126–131.
9. Sorensen, pp. 110, 111.
10. Public Law 86–90 — "Captive Nations Week Resolution," July 17, 1959.
11. See "Captive Nations Week Resolutions," 91st Congress, first session, Report No. 91–514, July 1969.
12. Dwight D. Eisenhower, *The White House Years: Waging Peace 1956–1961* (New York: Doubleday, 1965), pp. 278–279.
13. Pirsein, pp. 406–407.
14. Sorensen, pp. 235, 236.

4

1961–63: New Heights of Support

John F. Kennedy probably had a greater interest in, and became more closely involved with, the U.S. information effort than any president up until that time. Kennedy and his closest advisors, like General Maxwell Taylor, were determined to expunge any surviving elements of "massive retaliation," with its concentration on big nuclear conflict. From Khrushchev's long address to the Soviet Central Committee on January 6, 1961, the incoming U.S. leaders believed the Soviets were similarly ready to seek much more limited forms of conflict. "Wars of national liberation," in communist jargon, seemed to characterize the future. The Kennedy team was confident that such conflicts, with their emphasis on winning hearts and minds, would offer the United States a good shot at using its information and psychological resources to great advantage.

Between Election Day, 1960 and the inauguration, Kennedy ordered several committees and individuals to study foreign affairs, especially information problems. After the inauguration he brought in as Director of USIA Edward R. Murrow, probably the best known public figure to have held the post.

After initially declaring his policy to be "the rugged truth," Murrow soon came to believe that USIA should perform a much stronger function than it had under George Allen in the Eisenhower administration. Murrow said that USIA should strive to persuade, not merely inform. He also felt that it should aggressively advise the President and the executive departments on the foreign *public opinion* aspects of U.S. foreign policies. In the latter conviction he was strongly supported by the administration. Murrow was authorized to attend all National Security Council meetings, and Kennedy frequently called on him to attend other important emergency meetings on international problems. Kennedy had a special phone installed to Murrow's desk (which Murrow called "the blow torch").

Murrow and Kennedy agreed that a new formal Statement of Mission for USIA was necessary to sharpen the definitions of the earlier Eisenhower statement. Published in January 1963, it stated that, "The Mission of the USIA is to help achieve United States foreign policy objectives. . . ." Thomas Sorensen, a top aide to Murrow at the time, writes that USIA was directed to accomplish its mission in two ways: "By 'influencing public attitudes in other nations' (not just disseminating information), and by 'Advising the President, his representatives abroad,' and the various departments 'on the implications of foreign opinion for present and contemplated' U.S. policies and programs."[1]

Murrow later elaborated on these ideas in testimony before Congress by saying, "persuasion is one of the most important" instruments of American power. "Our arsenal of persuasion must be as ready as our nuclear arsenal, and used as never before."[2]

During the Kennedy years, the nation suffered several international setbacks and crises that tested the ability of USIA to handle an international information program. Soon after Kennedy took office, the Bay of Pigs operation was launched in Cuba. The resulting fiasco initiated a major period of trial for all the information agencies. Later in 1961, Soviet violations of the informal moratorium on atmospheric nuclear testing, which had been in effect since 1958, were discovered. The

Soviets in fact set off a series of 40 blasts in the atmosphere. Murrow was instrumental in persuading Kennedy to hold off announcing an American decision to resume tests for several months in order to capitalize on the propaganda benefits accruing from the Soviet violations.[3] The same year also witnessed the erection of the Berlin Wall by the Soviets. Then, in 1962 the Cuban missile crisis erupted, with the subsequent naval quarantine around the island, nuclear tensions, and the eventual Soviet concessions.

All of these events strained the Voice's ability to maintain an even-handed level of broadcasting the facts while simultaneously striving to promote and assist U.S. policy. Some members of the Voice staff would later complain that they had been required to do nothing more than "whitewash" American foreign policy. Thus again, the lines were being drawn between the "objectivity" and "mission" points of view.

Support for the Voice from Congress reached a new peak during the Kennedy-Murrow years. Fulfilling the goals of the Eisenhower modernization plan, the budgets rose from $17 million in fiscal 1960 to $27 million in 1964. There were also major additions to the physical facilities.[4]

In attempting to focus attention on specific American foreign policy objectives, USIA began to direct its activities towards specific target audience groups overseas. The Public Affairs Officers in the embassies were directed to tailor their efforts so as to articulate well-defined objectives to a particular audience. The Voice also made greater efforts along these lines, similar to the RIAS approach, of addressing concrete groups in East Germany (farmers, labor, youth, women, etc.). The Voice, for example, began broadcasting a special program for young people in 18 languages, entitled "The World We Live In."[5]

Radio Free Europe and Radio Liberty also received additional financial support (still channeled through the CIA). Their budgets rose from $20.9 million in fiscal 1960 to $25.6 million in 1964. Their policies reflected the continuing strong anti-communist mind-set that had carried over from the Eisenhower to the Kennedy administration. Since they were still only clandestinely supported by the government, they received only indirect policy guidance from the State Department and had not yet developed the split between the "news" and "policy" factions that had emerged in the Voice.

By now the staffs at RFE/RL had long since given up any proclivity to actively encourage "liberation." (As noted, the name of Radio Liberation was changed to Radio Liberty in December 1963.) But broadcasts were still following an active policy of encouraging nonviolent efforts to bring about greater freedom and the reduction of rigid central government controls in the communist countries. In 1963 the Director of Radio Free Europe, C. Rodney Smith, summarized the policies of RFE in a lengthy memorandum. This document included many ideas that were being expressed in the USIA, including Murrow's exhortation to develop better methods of persuasion, as well as USIA's efforts to direct its appeals to specific *groups* in the target audiences:

> The purpose of Radio Free Europe's broadcasting is, in accordance with U.S. policy, to help the peoples of these countries work toward freedom from Communist tyranny. Full independence under governments installed by free elections and responsive to the popular will is still, in spite of a generation of Communist brainwashing, the goal of the people in these captive nations. Radio Free Europe supports their peaceful struggle to reach this goal. . . .
> —The process starts with the breaking of the Communist monopoly over news and information.

> *Then RFE:*

> —brings hope through reporting and interpreting the facts of the broader trends and developments in the world.
> —strengthens the historic sense of identification of our audiences with *the West and Western values,* especially those of the Europe which they consider themselves a part.
> —persuades its audiences that the Communist system which rules them is not immune to change, that its promised world victory will not take place and that, on the contrary, they, as individuals and as members of groups, and as citizens of nations, have a vital—and peaceful—part to play in accelerating the defeat of the world Communist movement.

—encourages assertions of individual, group and national identity and self-interest in order to strengthen trends which in fact are today gradually eroding the grip of the Communist regimes over the people, and undermining Soviet control over the regimes themselves.

Within these general objective RFE is currently promoting:

I. A gradual revision of the Soviet satellites to a semi-market economy and a greater reliance on private property by;

(A) recording the success of the European Common Market as proof of the vitality of a market economy based on private property.

(B) promoting tourist, commercial and cultural contacts with the West in order to increase East European awareness of Western standards, products and technology.

(C) making it clear to the regimes that only by substantially increasing living standards can they secure from their captives' populations the minimum cooperation necessary for the successful operation of modern economics.

(D) convincing elite audiences that the most important single prerequisite of higher living standards is *more efficient agriculture and* that this in turn requires *greater emphasis on private plots*, the granting of increased incentives to the farmers and the gradual abandonment in fact, if not in name, of collectivized agriculture.

(E) persuading elite audiences that *centralized management of industry* is an increasing obstacle to high rates of economic growth, that even state-owned factories must be put on a profit and loss basis if enormous waste is to be avoided, and that it is absurd to attempt to operate a modern economy without the payment of interest, rent or profit.

II. The decline in the power and influence of the party apparatus; the emergency of other centers of power; and the gradual development of a genuine public opinion by:

(A) forcing *regime media*, through competitive broadcasting, to move toward their proper, as against their Communist role, of informing the public.

(B) supporting the *writer and artists* in their struggle to free themselves from the dictates of Socialist Realism, and to establish themselves as the "conscience of the nation," as a source of ideas and values increasingly independent of party control.

(C) promoting the establishment and growth of rudimentary forms of representative government....[6]

(Emphasis has been added to show some of the specific groups targeted.)

NOTES

1. Sorensen, p. 142.
2. Quoted in Sorensen, p. 145.
3. Sorensen, pp. 146, 147.
4. Pirsein, pp. 407–420.
5. Sorensen, pp. 143, 145, 195.
6. Internal RFE Memo of 9/5/63 given to the the author by General Smith.

5

1964–80: Detente and Growing
Controversies

Kennedy's administration came to its tragic end in November 1963. Murrow had to resign from USIA due to cancer in 1964 and died in 1965. President Lyndon B. Johnson appointed Carl Rowan as Director of USIA to succeed Murrow. Rowan was credited with doing an effective administrative job, but he never gained the close relationship with the President, nor did he wield the influence on foreign policy formulation that Murrow had. Although Rowan was authorized to attend National Security Council meetings, he did not receive the attention nor did he attempt to match the bureaucratic influence of his illustrious predecessor.

United States international broadcasting, under Johnson and Rowan, entered a sixteen year period in which financial and other support steadily declined. This decline can be traced to a number of domestic and foreign policy factors, but under Johnson, two were dominant: (1) the President placed less emphasis on international information than had Kennedy, and (2) the administration was soon to be plagued by the first signs since World War II of major disagreements over foreign policy among the public and in Congress and the administration. The war in Vietnam was emerging as an all-consuming source of controversy, and defense policy overshadowed concerns about broadcasting. Johnson and Defense Secretary Robert Mc-Namara initiated a calculated policy of allowing the Soviets to catch up with our nuclear arsenal, believing that after the Soviets attained strategic parity, further arms control agreements would naturally follow. Both trends led to some diminution of a strong information policy against Soviet policy and ideology.

Rowan, however, was highly adamant about the subject of official "policy" guidance over the Voice. Murrow had directed the Voice to follow administration policy but had been relatively flexible in exerting day-to-day operational control. By March 1965, Henry Loomis, one of the authors of the Voice Charter, was becoming uneasy under Rowan and resigned.

The circumstances surrounding Loomis' resignation display striking parallels to the controversies that would plague the Voice sixteen years later when the Reagan Administration was attempting to revise VOA policy. In both instances, there was an invocation of the Voice Charter and a major leak to the press.

Loomis made a farewell speech to the staff in which he said that "during my seven years, we at the Voice have largely reached a consensus on how best to apply this Charter to our day to day programming . . . . It is my hope, my belief, that the Charter, like the Constitution, is so fundamental and so represents the realities of the world and the moral principles that undergird this nation, that the Charter will endure for the life of the Voice. . . . Perhaps most fundamental of all, we believe our audience judges us as a radio, while some of our colleagues assume that the audience considers a commentary on the Voice as authoritative a statement of United States policy as a statement by the Secretary of State or the President. . . . To sweep under the rug what we don't like, what does not serve our tactical purpose, is a sign of weakness."[1]

According to Thomas Sorensen, an outside reporter, Mary McGrory, was invited to the staff meeting and was "briefed" on its significance. She wrote in the *Washington Star* that "everyone present . . . knew what he meant. . . .

Old-timers in the Voice say they are going through a period almost as bad as the McCarthy era. . . . every commentary must be cleared with the policy department of the Voice's parent agency. . . ." Needless to say, top USIA Officials and Johnson were angry over this newspaper report on an internal meeting.[2]

Meanwhile, controversies were also arising across the country over American foreign policy in general, and, for the first time, over Vietnam in particular. 1965 was the year in which the first tremors could be heard that would split in the United States over its role in Vietnam. These disagreements echoed in the organizational rivalries within the Voice over treatment of news.

In August 1965, Johnson persuaded John Chancellor to take Loomis' old spot as Director of the Voice, making Chancellor the first professional newsman to hold the position. Rowan resigned from USIA and was succeeded by Leonard Marks, a Washington lawyer with years of experience representing broadcasters legally, but a with little additional communications background. Marks had represented Lyndon Johnson's broadcasting interests for years and had a good personal relationship with the President.

Chancellor's professionalism combined with Marks' pragmatism produced a relationship that ended the quarrels between the broadcasters and the policy makers, at least during their respective tenures. Chancellor issued a firm standing order that the Policy Office should clear all commentaries. He tried to keep the policy officers from dictating the content of hard news stories, and his good judgment reduced the complaints that previously emanated from the Policy Office. One such officer said, "We still can't lay down the law on what VOA says on its newscasts, but we don't have to anymore."[3] Unfortunately for the Voice, Chancellor resigned in 1967 to return to private industry. He was succeeded by John Daly, another professional broadcaster. Under Daly, the latent battles over "policy" versus "objectivity" began to simmer under the surface again, as the situation in Vietnam began to polarize the nation.[4]

The ever-increasing domestic strife caused by the American

involvement in Vietnam had predictable consequences for USIA, and for the Voice in particular. Since Daly believed in continuing Chancellor's concern for objectivity in broadcasts, he felt obligated to have Voice programs report on the dissension within the United States over Vietnam. Congressional critics intensified their assaults on this policy. Representative Charles Joleson (D–N.J.) announced, "The Voice of America is to promulgate our Government policy. If that policy is wrong, we ought to change it here, not broadcast statements opposing that policy."[5]

Though Rowan was committed to win the war of ideas in Vietnam, the lack of coordination afflicting broader political, military, and diplomatic decisions in the administration and congress precluded a sustained, successful information program. Rowan was assigned by Johnson to administer all psychological operations in Vietnam, and he established a Joint U.S. Public Affairs Office (JUSPAO) in Saigon. Headed by former VOA Program Manager Barry Zorthian, JUSPAO combined USIA communications experts with Pentagon psychological operations officers and other media specialists.[6] After a promising start, the office eventually suffered from internal divisions, lack of adequate funding, and the general lack of a cohesive mission.

By 1968 controversies in the United States over Vietnam were coming to a boil. The TET Offensive in the Spring of 1968 resulted in a military disaster for the communists but was played up as a defeat for the United States by many American and other journalists. President Johnson announced that he would not run again. The ensuing Democratic Convention, accompanied by the riots in Chicago, and the presidential campaign between Hubert Humphrey and Richard Nixon further exacerbated the differences in the country over the war. All these events created difficult problems for the Voice in transmitting news and commentaries and led ultimately to a more cautious broadcasting policy.

The year 1968 also saw one development that provided dramatic evidence of the power of free ideas within the closed societies of Eastern Europe. This was the year of the "Prague Spring" in Czechoslovakia. For five years there had been a gradual thaw in the rigid Stalinist control mechanisms in Czechoslovakia, culminating in the appointment of Alexander Dubcek as First Secretary of the Czechoslovakian Communist Party in January 1968. The Dubcek regime promulgated a number of economic and cultural reforms transforming Czechoslovakia into the most liberal Warsaw Pact member state. The country's radio, TV, and press all flourished under the Dubcek reforms.

The process of liberalization in Prague caused increasing concern in Moscow and other Eastern European capitals. Diplomatic pressures from the Soviets, and Dubcek's persistant refusal to halt the reform process, eventually led to an invasion of Czechoslovakia in August 1968 by Soviet and all other Warsaw Pact armies (except Rumania), employing more tanks than had been used by the Red Army to invade Germany at the end of World War II. The Dubcek government was forcibly ousted and replaced by a regime servile to the Soviets. Dubcek himself was retained as a figurehead for several months and was not officially replaced until April 1969.

Once again, the painful dilemma of 1953 and 1956 confronted the Radios. Although there is little direct evidence that American broadcasts were influential in instigating the "Prague Spring," it seems likely that the information provided over the years by VOA, RFE, and other Western broadcasts were important in keeping the ideas of freedom alive in Czechoslovakia. Yet, when idea became action, the West could do little to help. Communist propagandists themselves blamed Western radios for many of their difficulties. In May 1968 Radio Moscow denounced "imperialist propaganda" coming into Czechoslovakia from the West. In May, the Dubcek government ceased jamming of all "officially recognized" Western broadcasting. RFE broadcasts were still subject to jamming, as they were not considered official. Meanwhile, the Soviets increased their broadcasting to Czechoslovakia from two half-hour programs per day to 168 hours per week. For the first time since 1950, Poland reinstated external broadcasts in Czech and Slovak for 140 hours per week, and Hungary also commenced broadcasts in Czech.[7]

It is interesting that RFE surveys during this period showed that the estimated RFE audience in Czechoslovakia rose from around 33% of the population in 1962 to a peak of 51% at the end of 1967. But during the first half of 1968, after Dubcek eased the restrictions on the media within the country, the RFE audience dropped down again to 37%, indicating that the population felt they were receiving more adequate news from internal sources. Audience coverage rose again to 65% immediately after the invasion. By 1971, when jamming had become even more severe, it had declined once more to 45%.[8]

In January 1969 President Richard Nixon took office. It was expected that his administration would conduct a radical overhaul in the country's information program, but in fact the changes implemented by Nixon were not as drastic as had been forecast. Nixon appointed Frank Shakespeare to be Director of USIA. Shakespeare had been second in command at CBS and also managed Nixon's television advertising campaign during the 1968 election. Shakespeare was known as a conservative with firm opinions about the global ambitions of the Soviets. Many of the USIA staff expected an attempt to politicize the agency, sharpen ideological content, and generally move USIA to the right. Shakespeare did launch a vigorous effort to provide more balance in USIA activities, directing, for example, USIA libraries around the world to order books by conservative authors in addition to those by liberals. But he also developed a reputation for fairness. He ordered an end to the old rule that public affairs officers overseas had to justify in writing orders for books critical of American life or policy.[9]

Kenneth Giddens, an Alabama businessman and owner of a highly successful TV station, was brought in as Director of VOA. He was also believed to be conservative but quickly developed a smooth relationship with the professional staff. He put through a number of measures to strengthen the news operation and launched a major effort to upgrade the physical equipment, much of which was already suffering from obsolescence.[10] Giddens later enhanced his reputation with the newsroom during the Watergate affair by resisting the efforts of the White House to have news of Watergate kept off the Voice. Although he had been a Nixon supporter, Giddens insisted that the Voice had to transmit news of the crisis as it developed in order to maintain its own credibility.[11]

Giddens also urged that the four-paragraph Voice Charter drawn up 13 years earlier under Henry Loomis and Barry Zorthian be made official to give the Voice a formal guide as to its mission. Shakespeare concurred before leaving office in 1973. Three years later, this Charter was incorporated in Public Law 94-350 by Congress.[12] Many in the Voice who later invoked this Charter in support of their views on "objectivity" may have been unaware that it had been promulgated in 1959 and made official in 1973 by two "conservatives" responsible for Voice policy.

Shakespeare also made progress in enhancing the activities of USIA in countering communist propaganda in the Third World. But although he and Giddens succeeded in revitalizing VOA news operations and increasing the budget for transmitters, there were fewer changes made in the content of broadcasts to the Soviet bloc. Nixon had long-established anticommunist credentials, but his administration soon launched a series of measures leading to the dramatic detente agreements of 1972. He appointed Henry Kissinger as National Security Advisor and later as Secretary of State. Kissinger was skillful in communicating with the press in the United States and also in Western Europe and the Third World. Shakespeare did much to improve the performance of USIA in relating to the media representatives in countries outside the Iron Curtain, assigning the ablest people to press relations offices in the most important countries.[13] Such capabilities of Kissinger and the USIA with the press were, of course, of little value in the communist countries, where the media are simply organs of the government.

Detente had predictable effects on all the Radios. Though Nixon and Kissinger supported budget increases for transmission facilities at the Radios, they were far less interested in the content of the broadcasts. In the memoirs of both men, there is no mention of the USIA, VOA, or the Radios. The primary emphasis of the Nixon administration was on diplomatic negotiations, balance of power problems, and scaling back

American overseas commitments. Any effort to contain or roll back communism via broadcasting took a very subordinate position.

Kissinger placed great emphasis on promoting the arms control accords and the opening to mainland China. Both initiatives resulted in further modifications of anti-communist rhetoric by the Voice and RFE/RL. Within the Radios, this trend, in turn, tended to favor the "news and objectivity" faction against the "policy" faction. Veterans of RFE/RL now say that more restrictions on comments critical of the communist powers were placed on them by Kissinger than by any top administration officials before or since.[14]

The Captive Nations Proclamations issued during Nixon's administration further exemplify its caution about policy toward the Soviet bloc. These annual proclamations had been gradually watered down since the original resolution signed by Eisenhower in 1959. Many in the Captive Nations movement had expected Nixon to return to a stronger line, but the yearly proclamations indicated little substantive change. The first, in 1969, a year after the Soviet invasion of Czechoslovakia, makes only passing reference to "Eastern Europe" and expresses America's "continued desire" for independence there. It mentions the desire of the United States to "sustain" with "understanding and sympathy" the just aspirations of the peoples of all nations. There is no longer any reference to Soviet aggression or repression in Czechoslovakia or elsewhere.

Growing controversy in the nation over Vietnam, with an assist from communist propagandists, led to a major upheaveal in RFE/RL in 1971. Senator Clifford Case (R–N.J.) rose on the floor of the Senate in January to announce that the Radios were being secretly funded by the CIA and stated his intention to introduce legislation to have them funded by Congressional appropriation, subject to Congressional oversight.

The CIA funding had not in fact been a secret for several years. It was mentioned by many in the news media as well as in Sorensen's book *The Word War*, published three years earlier. But Case's announcement opened the floodgates for all those opposed to a clandestinely-supported radio operation against the communists. Senator J. William Fulbright, (D–Ark.) Chairman of the Senate Foreign Relations Committee, said that the Radios as well as RIAS in Berlin were "relics of the cold war" and that their continued operation would harm Nixon's policy of detente. The speeches of both Case and Fulbright received extensive coverage in the media, accompanied by much editorial sentiment for the elimination of the Radios. The links to the CIA provided additional ammunition to opponents, allowing them to tie into the campaign in Congress and the media against CIA "crimes" and "abuses."

There is evidence that at this point the Soviets and their allies were becoming much more concerned about the impact of RFE/RL, and had launched an active campaign to put them out of action. The Soviets had, of course, attacked the Radios regularly since their founding in the early 1950s, but the attacks had become stronger and more systematic in 1968, the year of the Prague Spring. In the shock of the Dubcek reforms, the Soviets and their Warsaw Pact allies mounted a more vigorous propaganda and subversive attack on the Radios.[15] There were meetings in Warsaw, Prague, East Berlin, and Moscow in 1969 and 1970 to discuss "Problems of Psychological Warfare Waged Against the Socialist States by the Mass Media of Imperialism." Soviet propagandists were instructed to stress the concept of peaceful coexistence to convince the West to renounce "ideological warfare," or to plan countermeasures.

The Warsaw Pact nations took up the cudgels with a vigorous campaign against Western radios, singling out RFE/RL, as being contrary to the spirit of detente. East German media organs spearheaded these attacks, calling on the West German government to cease permitting these stations to broadcast from German territory, since they were "relics of the cold war." This phrase was used by the East German media two years before its use by Senator Fulbright.[16]

The East bloc nations also stepped up their clandestine efforts against the Radios in the United States. A secret detachment was organized in Poland in 1970 with considerable financial resources to launch disinformation activities in the United States under the direction of Soviet advisers. The Premier of Poland sent letters to the President of West Germany

and President Nixon urging them in the interests of better relations to put an end to the "cold war" activities of RFE. A
Polish double agent who had succeeded in getting a job at RFE
for several years returned to Warsaw and began to publish
exaggerated stories about the "espionage" activities of the
Radio.[17]

A newspaper column by Rowland Evans and Robert Novak
in April 1972 reported more details on the communist effort
to kill the Radios, operating through the Polish Communist
Party. The column stated that the Polish unit had a budget of
$3 million and worked through the Polish Embassy in Wash-
ington.[18]

As a result of Senator Case's revelations, Nixon appointed a
commission under the direction of Milton Eisenhower in August 1972 to investigate the Radios and to recommend action.
Cord Meyer wrote that he was convinced that Case did not
want to see the Radios eliminated, but was is not so certain
about the motives of Case's principal assistant working on this
subject, John Marks. Marks later resigned from Case's staff and
cooperated with Philip Agee, the CIA defector, in his work
exposing CIA agents and activities around the world.[19]

As Congress debated the issue of support for the Radios, the
communist propaganda drive against them continued unabated. Later in 1972, a commando unit broke into the house
of the editor of the largest U.S. Polish daily newspaper in Chicago and stole files, including two letters from Jan Nowak, the
head of the RFE Polish service in Munich. A few weeks later
the press in Poland published these two letters along with a
third, a forgery. Copies of all three letters were somehow furnished to Senator Fulbright. The letters contained derogatory
references to Senators Fulbright and Case, thus making Fulbright and his supporters even more negative about the Radios.[20]

The attacks on the Radios by Fulbright and his followers,
however, seemed to bring to life a large amount of latent support in Congress, the media, and the public. This support received additional stimulus from the revelations of the
undercover communist campaign, as described in the Evans
and Novak column.

The Eisenhower Commission issued its report in February 1973, entitled "The Right to Know," containing a strong recommendation for the continuation of the Radios, but without any links to the CIA.

The Commission concluded that the Radios could "contribute to a climate of detente rather than detract from it." The report said further, "Experience in the last few months has shown that 'relaxation of tensions' on the government level (in communist countries) does not necessarily lead to a relaxation of internal controls. In fact since the summer of 1972, just the opposite has occurred. We therefore recommend that the stations be continued until the governments of the countries to which the stations are broadcasting permit a free flow of information and ideas. . . ." Considering that the nation was still in the aftermath of the 1972 spirit, these were notable conclusions.

In order to provide a structure that would preserve the professional independence of the Radios, as well as to ensure that broadcasts would not be entirely inconsistent with U.S. foreign policy, the Commission recommended the formation of a Board for International Broadcasting (BIB) as an independent public institution. This board would perform the following functions:

— receive Congressional appropriations and make grants to the Radios;

— be responsible for assuring that the stations "do not operate in a manner inconsistent with broad United States foreign policy objectives."

— be vigilant on behalf of the professional integrity of the Radios;

— be responsible for the fiscal controls and effective use of funds.

The Boards of Directors of both Radios were retained, thus creating a potential overlapping of functions with the BIB that was to cause continual problems in the future.[21]

The report received substantial support in Congress. A Board for International Broadcasting Act incorporating the provisions of the report was passed by both Houses and signed by the President, taking effect in October 1973 as Public Law 93-129.

The BIB reports directly to the President, through the National Security Council. It is independent of the State Department and the USIA in line with the Eisenhower Commission's recommendation that the independent status of the Radios should be maintained. Public Law 93-129 specified only that the Secretary of State "shall provide the board with such information regarding the foreign policy of the United States that the Secretary may deem appropriate." Thus the Secretary of State has only an advisory function. The lines of authority for the USIA, VOA, and the BIB are summarized in Figure 1.

So the Radios survived, but the often heated debate in Congress caused considerable damage to morale at both Radios. For more than a year, the staffs were kept in the dark about their future status, future budget support, and general direction of broadcasting policy. During this period, therefore, there was an inevitable tendency among the staffs to become more cautious in their approach to ideological content. In 1972, for example, *The New York Times Magazine* ran an article by Henry Kamm describing the attacks on the Radios in Congress and the media, including interviews with staff members in Munich. One statement to Kamm by the head of the Hungarian desk was revealing. "We in RFE," he said, "are not asking the Communists to give up Communism. Friends who have been to Hungary tell me they believe Socialism is now generally accepted in the country. I don't wish it, but one must accept reality. I am not entitled by the Hungarian people to represent or lead them. I have no mandate from anybody. I am not the Voice of Free Hungary or the Hungarian conscience. We don't broadcast the views of Hungarian emigré politicians because they live in the past. We have to be realistic. We would like a beautiful Communism, or as Khrushchev said, a goulash Communism."[22]

This statement was strongly condemned by many in the Hungarian-American community in this country, which has

Figure 1

LINES OF AUTHORITY OF U.S. BROADCASTING ORGANIZATIONS

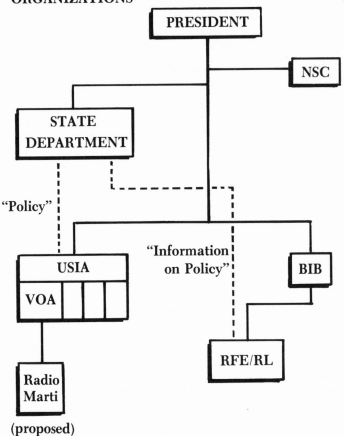

(proposed)

The Voice of America, as a division of the United States Information Agency, reports to the Executive Office of the President, and receives policy direction from the State Department.

The Board for International Broadcasting, which has authority over RFE/RL, also reports directly to the Executive Office of the President. According to Public Law 93-129 of October 19, 1973 establishing the BIB, its relationship to the Secretary of State is defined as follows:

To assist the Board in carrying out its functions, the Secretary of State shall provide the Board with such information regarding the foreign policy of the United States as the Secretary may deem appropriate.

NOTE: Solid lines indicate direct authority. Dotted lines indicate indirect guidance.

mounted a continuous campaign of criticism of RFE Hungarian broadcasts ever since.[23]

Under Nixon and then Gerald Ford, the State Department had begun the long, tortuous negotiations with the Soviets that resulted in the Agreement on Security and Cooperation in Europe, or the Helsinki Final Act of August 1, 1975. This document was signed by the United States, Canada, and all the countries of Europe, with the exception of Albania.[24]

Leonid Brezhnev had been working for this agreement for years as a means of gaining legitimacy for the postwar boundaries and the communist governments of Eastern Europe. In return for provisions ensuring the sanctity of European borders, Brezhnev agreed to sections that appeared to guarantee greater human rights in Europe: freedom to travel, reunification of families, freedom of press and religion, scientific and cultural exchanges, economic cooperation, and reduction of jamming. Critics of the agreement said that it was so vaguely worded in diplomatic language that it was a dubious guarantee of any of these rights.[25] The provision regarding jamming of broadcasts read as follows:

> The participating states note the expansion in the dissemination of information broadcast by radio, and express the hope for a continuation of this process, so as to meet the interest of mutual understanding among peoples and the aims set forth by this Conference[26]

In fact, the Soviets never reduced jamming operations in the wake of the Helsinki accords.

In December 1975 one of Kissinger's senior advisers, Helmut Sonnenfeldt, presided over a meeting of U.S. ambassadors in London and issued a statement on conditions in Eastern Europe, which implicitly clarified the mission of American broadcasting. The statement read in part, "In today's circumstances neither side (the United Sates nor the Soviet Union) can gain a strategic advantage that can be translated into political utility. We are doomed to co-existence." The implication of this statement, according to British political analyst Brian Crozier, was that the United States must strive for a more organic relationship between Eastern Europe and the Soviet Union, with greater national autonomy within the context of a strong Soviet geopolitical influence.[27]

This "Sonnenfeldt Doctrine," as it was dubbed, thus seemed to imply that Eastern Europe was the natural Soviet sphere of influence, and that the United States, in the interests of peace and stability, should not seek actively to persuade the people of those countries to reject Soviet hegemony. The statement naturally had its effects on the policies of Radio Free Europe. Eventually, criticisms of the communist governments and the Soviet power behind them became rarer, and the political commentary in general became blander.

Since its establishment in 1973, the Board for International Broadcasting had been studying the relative costs and benefits of merging various functions of RFE and RL. The Eisenhower Commission had originally examined the feasibility of merging the two organizations and decided against it, stating that, "Each of the two Radios had developed a commendable esprit, an expertise, control systems, and operations that would be disrupted for a considerable time."[28] Nevertheless, during 1974-76, the BIB and the management of the two stations proceeded to carry out mergers, first of the administrative and financial functions, and finally of the entire programming apparatus. These moves were all made in the interests of economy, and there is no doubt that they did bring about considerable savings in duplicated expenses. But the eventual merger of the programming functions had one result that has been controversial ever since: the elimination of the Radio Liberty newsroom. This was merged into the Radio Free Europe newsroom, which in effect did away with Radio Liberty's previous method of operating. As described earlier, the RL newsroom had operated by a different procedure from RFE.

The RL newsroom selected its news according to a rather narrow criteria of what was interesting for an audience within Russia and spent a considerable amount of time editing news for a Russian audience. The RFE newsroom, by contrast, selected its items more broadly from a menu of international news and passed it along to the five different language desks. When the two newsrooms were merged, the Russian desk of the new combined organization now received a news package from the same Central Newsroom that supplied stories to the five Eastern European language desks. All of the original selection and editing done especially for the Russian audience was eliminated. Critics since that time have argued that this move had a serious effect on the quality of the broadcasts to the Soviet Union. They contend that this is one reason for the decline in the audience coverage in the Soviet Union since 1976.[29]

President Jimmy Carter took office in January 1977. His administration initially sought to accelerate the trend toward detente, causing further changes in the information program in the direction of more "dialogue" with the Soviet bloc countries. Broadcasting programs to counter communist ideology, support for liberation, or even any efforts to encourage greater peaceful efforts to bring about popular pressures for more democratic institutions in communist countries, virtually disappeared at the Radios and the Voice.

Although there was no formal statement, the new administration's conception of the Soviet Union and its objectives seemed to be that the U.S.S.R. was a major power that we could live with peacefully if we could enhance mutual understanding. President Carter, in his seminal Notre Dame speech in June 1977, set the tone by saying that we have overcome our "inordinate fear of communism."

The emphasis in American information policy was placed on trying to build bridges, to encourage better U.S.-Soviet understanding, and to share ideas. The information agencies would still attempt to explain our policies but would stay away from encouraging any actions towards greater liberties in the U.S.S.R. and Eastern Europe.

Symbolically, the name of the United States Information Agency was changed to the U.S. International Communication Agency (USICA) in April 1978. The plaque on the outside of the Headquarters building in Washington was changed, and the old slogan, "Telling America's Story," disappeared with it. These actions were subtle but significant, indications of the new emphasis on two-way "communications" and the exchange of ideas rather than on one-way persuasion. The new

USICA assumed responsibility for the Bureau of Educational and Cultural Affairs, previously under the State Department Office, which handled the Exchange of Persons Program and other cultural efforts abroad.

At the opening ceremonies in April, the new USICA Director, John Reinhardt, quoted President Carter in setting the keynote for the new organization. Carter had said, "Only by knowing and understanding each other's experience can we find common ground on which we can examine and resolve our differences." Reinhardt went on to say "It is also imperative that other societies know clearly where we stand and why — as a government and as a people — on issues of concern. An important part of our mandate is the obligation to explain American policies as clearly and effectively as we can."[30]

The BIB announced guidelines for applying these objectives to the Radios. In its annual report for 1978, BIB defined the mission of the Radios as "to encourage a constructive *dialogue* with the peoples of the U.S.S.R. and Eastern Europe." (Emphasis added.)[31]

The BIB and the Radios followed the guidelines but ran into difficulties in implementing a "two-way" dialogue. Communist jamming of the Radios continued in spite of provisions in the Final Act of the Helsinki accord which called for "expansion in the dissemination of information broadcast by radio." The BIB and USICA asked the American delegation to raise the issue at a conference held in Belgrade in September 1977 to review compliance with the Helsinki agreement. The United States was joined by other Western nations in this protest, but the jamming continued. What was more, the Soviets accused the Radios themselves of being contrary to the spirit of Helsinki by broadcasting "defamatory propaganda."

The BIB rejected this charge in its 1978 annual report and in consonance with its communication objectives made the following proposals to the Soviet bloc countries:

> Over the past two years, it has been suggested to several of the East European governments that they call to the Board's attention specific broadcasts which in their view were inaccurate or overstepped generally accepted standards of fair comment. The Board

remains pledged to receive and investigate any such complaints in the future, as it has in the past.

However, very few specific complaints have been brought to the attention of the Board by officials of the countries to which RFE/RL broadcasts. We restate our willingness to investigate their complaints whenever they believe a program has violated our Statement of Mission, the Program Policy Guidelines of RFE/RL or the Final Act. Moreover, the Board is prepared seriously to consider, in concert with the Radios, the development of procedures for making RFE/RL airtime available to officials of the Soviet Union and Eastern Europe for responses to those specific complaints which have merit. No radio enterprise broadcasting 980 hours a week can avoid committing an occasional inaccuracy. It would be eminently more sensible for the governments involved to develop, in cooperation with the Board, an orderly way to correct such lapses when they occur, rather than to engage indiscriminately in a costly jamming exercise which violates the very essence of the Helsinki commitment to the free flow of information.[32]

The statement embodied the operating assumption that the communist countries might reciprocate the U.S. interest in encouraging a "dialogue," and that they might allow us to communicate more freely with their people as long as they had the privilege of correcting occasional "inaccuracies."

The BIB was never able to work out any such arrangement with the communist governments, and even more moderate programming by RFE/RL was met by unabated jamming. In fact, the jamming of Radio Liberty in European Russia became more severe in 1979 and 1980 (jamming of VOA in the U.S.S.R. was resumed in August 1980).

The policy of attempting bilateral communication, nevertheless, led to a further accentuation of the trend in the Radios and the Voice to avoid critiques of the communist system, to minimize attempts to encourage peaceful progress towards democratic institutions, and to put increasing emphasis on "objectivity" in the news.

By 1980 there had begun to be some disillusionment within the Carter administration over detente, after a number of foreign policy disasters:

— The upheavals in Iran, ousting of the Shah, and the seizure of the hostages, all encouraged by blatant propaganda broadcasts from Soviet soil, augmented by the
concentration of Soviet troops on the Soviet-Iranian border.
— Angola's invasion of Zaire. Carter blamed Cuba for
training the Angolan troops but was later unable to document the charge adequately.
— Detection of a Soviet "brigade" in Cuba.
— The bloody events unfolding in Afghanistan, culminating in the Soviet invasion. Carter imposed a partial grain
embargo and said his concept of Soviet intentions had
changed more in the two weeks following this invasion
than in his entire previous experience.

Another factor in the growing doubts about detente was the
ongoing and intensive Soviet propaganda campaign. In spite
of the statements of communist leaders for foreign consumption about peace and detente, the propaganda organs in the
U.S.S.R. continued to feed their own people a line identical
to that of earlier years. This familiar line portrayed the United
States and the other democracies as bourgeois exploiters of the
working masses at home, and as imperialists abroad, pursuing
a policy of aggression and bellicosity. Much of this rhetoric
was also used in Soviet propaganda to the Third World; it also
appeared with increasing frequency at the UN and UNESCO,
which was promoting governmental control of foreign reporting from Third World countries.

NOTES

1. Henry Loomis, "Remarks made by Henry Loomis on the Occasion of his Departure as Director, Voice of America, USIA,"
HEW Auditorium, Washington, D.C., March 4, 1965.
2. Sorensen, p. 241.
3. Ibid., p. 245.
4. Ibid., pp. 246–249.

5. Browne, *International Radio Broadcasting*, p. 105.
6. Sorensen, p. 281.
7. Burton Paulu, *Radio and Television Broadcasting in Eastern Europe*, (Minneapolis: University of Minnesota Press, 1974) pp. 320, 321.
8. Paulu, pp. 355–356.
9. *Time*, December 6, 1969, p. 40; *Newsweek*, February 12, 1970, p. 20.
10. Interviews with a veteran VOA news desk editor and a former top USIA officer.
11. Hanu, op. cit., pp. 41–43.
12. Ibid., p. 42.
13. Interview with former USIA official, one of Shakespeare's principal aides, May 1983.
14. Interviews with VOA and RFE/RL East European desks editors and writers, July–August 1982.
15. Gerhard Wetting *Broadcasting and Detente*, (New York: St. Martin's Press, 1977), pp. 12, 13.
16. Ibid.
17. Ibid., p. 34.
18. "Poles Aid Drive Against RFE," Washington Post 4/23/72.
19. Meyer, p. 135.
20. Wetting, pp. 37, 38. For further discussion, see pp. 39–41.
21. *The Right to Know*, Report of the Presidential Study Commission on International Radio Broadcasting, (Washington, D.C.: GPO, 2/5/73), pp. 38–40.
22. Henry Kamm, "Radio Free Europe, The In Sound from Outside," *N.Y. Times Magazine*, 9/26/72, p. 37.
23. Interviews with several Americans of Hungarian descent in the U.S.
24. Henry Kissinger, *Years of Upheaval*, (Boston: Little Brown and Company, 1982) p. 1.
25. *Current History*, October 1975, pp. 143, 144; *U.S. News and World Report*, August 4, 1975, pp. 14–18.
26. Quoted in *Second Annual Report 1975*, (Washington, D.C.: Board for International Broadcasting, October 30, 1975) p. 1.
27. Quoted in Brian Crozier, *Strategy of Survival*. (New Rochelle: Arlington House, 1978), p. 123.
28. *The Right to Know*, p. 47.
29. Sabur, p. 10.

30. Quoted in U.S. International Communication Agency, *Report to Congress 1978-1979*, (Washington, June 1980), p. 4.
31. Board for International Broadcasting, *Fourth Annual Report 1978*, (Washington, January 1978), p. 1.
32. Ibid., pp. 3, 4.

6
1981 to Date: The Search
for New Guidelines

The Reagan administration took office in January 1981 pledged to a stronger policy against communist ideology and Soviet aggressiveness. Reagan's inauguration represented a break with recent trends. The President as well as the new Secretary of State, Alexander Haig, made it clear that administration policy would be based on the assumption that the Soviets had not abandoned their historic designs of bringing about the communization of the world. They also stated that while the United States would not attempt to promote violent revolutions, it would be more active in countering Soviet propaganda and encouraging resistance to communist tyranny and peaceful change within the communist countries.

Secretary Haig outlined these aims in a speech before the Berlin Press Association in September 1981, marking the twentieth anniversary of the Berlin Wall. "Democracy has enabled us to create unprecedented opportunities for our citizens," he said. "But democracy is also the heritage of all men . . . . Repeated attempts at repression have left it stronger and more appealing than ever. I believe that the democratic revolution, with its proof in the performance of our own societies, is the-best hope for human progress. The democracies in the West have a unique privilege—and a compelling obligation—to promulgate their own revolutionary doctrine throughout the world."

Reagan summarized this policy in his speech before the British Parliament on June 8, 1982:

> . . . . Democracy is not a fragile flower; still it needs cultivating. If the rest of this century is to witness the gradual growth of freedom and democratic ideas, we must take action to assist the campaign for democracy. . . .
>
> While we must be cautious about forcing the pace of change, we must not hesitate to declare our ultimate objectives and to take concrete actions to move towards them. We must be staunch in our conviction that freedom is not the sole prerogative of a lucky few but the inalienable and universal right of all human beings. So states the U.N. Universal Declaration of Human Rights, which among other things, guarantees free elections.
>
> The objective I propose is quite simple to state: to foster the infrastructure of democracy — the system of a free press, unions, political parties, universities — which allow a people to choose their own way, to develop their own culture, to reconcile their own differences through peaceful means.

A key element of this policy of the new administration was to be a more active information program. As the director of USICA, Reagan appointed Charles Z. Wick, an old associate with a background in the communications and entertainment industries. As head of the Board for International Broadcasting, Reagan named Frank Shakespeare, President of RKO General and Director of USIA from 1969 to 1973. Shakespeare had always believed that the United States required an active information effort to offset communist censorship and propaganda.

The efforts of Wick and Shakespeare to bring about changes in the policies of the Voice and the Radios met difficulties almost immediately. Both organizations had built up managements over the years who resisted any policies of activist anti-communist broadcasts. This trend had been growing ever since the early years of the Johnson administration, so that the top echelons of both broadcasters were almost entirely committed to the policies of "informing" only, with little effort at "persuasion."

Differences between the objectives of the new administration and the policy assumptions of some of the broadcasting organizations' managers led to a number of controversies over policy in 1981 and 1982, many of which were covered in the American media. The next three chapters will touch on these controversies briefly, outline how they have been resolved to date, and describe the present situations at the broadcasting organizations under three headings: physical equipment, personnel, and programming policy.

Part II
PRESENT SITUATION

7

Physical Equipment

As a result of the low priority given to international broadcasting by U.S. administrations since the 1960s, the physical equipment of VOA and RFE/RL failed to grow and in many areas became obsolescent. The number of high power short-wave transmitters available to VOA has not exceeded 55 since 1973, while the total number of such transmitters operated by all countries worldwide has almost doubled, from 221 to 408. The failure to modernize transmission facilities is one of the more visible examples of America's declining position on the world's airwaves.

Much of the VOA and RFE/RL equipment is so outdated that one VOA language desk chief has called the equipment used by VOA reporters in the field nothing but "junk." He says broadcasting quality inevitably suffers as a result. A few years ago, he inquired as to why VOA broadcasts to Hungary were being received so poorly. After checking, VOA management gave him the reason for the weak signal: due to directional antenna changes, the Hungarian programs could best be heard in the vicinity of Warsaw.[1]

The House Foreign Affairs Committee in an April 2, 1982 report said that:

> Though U.S. arsenals of defense are stocked with state-of-the-art weaponry, the United States has neglected the technology of broadcasting and has relayed the nation's messages on transmitters which were the state-of-the-art in 1938.[2]

For example, the transmitters used by VOA in Munich were built by Joseph Goebbels' propaganda ministry and still employ vacuum tube technology. The main broadcasting studios of RFE/RL in Munich are in a building designed as a hospital in World War II. Unlike even the simplest facilities in the United States, these studios have no air conditioning and only primitive soundproofing. Many have windows facing the street, which results in the transmission of street noises.

In broadcasting to the communist countries, both VOA and RFE/RL are confronted by a tremendous jamming organization. As already noted, the Soviet bloc is estimated to spend about $300 million on jamming activities alone. This is almost 50% more than the worldwide broadcasting budgets of VOA and RFE/RL combined, including all programming and personnel, as well as transmission expenses. This huge Soviet outlay on electrical energy is devoted solely to the creation of *noise*, at a time when many parts of the Soviet bloc are suffering from energy shortages. In fact, in many of these countries consumers are frequently ordered to shut off their electrical appliances for several hours to conserve energy, at a time when their governments are pouring this energy into the atmosphere to prevent them from receiving news from abroad.

The Soviet Union also devotes a much larger budget to broadcasting, estimated to be about $700 million. This is more than three times that of VOA and RFE/RL combined. Comparisons here are difficult for several reasons. The Soviet Union actually spends much less in broadcasting to the United States and Western Europe than America spends in broadcasting to the Soviet bloc. The Soviets know that shortwave broadcasts have a very small audience in the Western democracies and that there is very little interest in listening to communist propaganda on the air. Western broadcasts to the Soviet Union, however, are another matter. Here the United States provides a source of information to populations that are victims of the tightest censorship on all infomration. Western broadcasts, therefore, could potentially attract large audiences and so are subjected to a huge jamming effort.

Communist broadcast efforts to the rest of the world, however, greatly exceed those of the democracies. The transmitting stations of VOA and RFE/RL total 151. The Soviet Union alone, in contrast, has 285 shortwave transmitters, excluding those of the other Eastern European countries and Cuba, which regularly cooperate with Radio Moscow in transmitting broadcasts. In addition, there are 123 medium and longwave transmitters in the Soviet Union within 500 miles of the Soviet borders that can reach other countries.

A breakdown of transmitters in terms of power illustrates an even greater margin of Soviet superiority. The U.S.S.R. has 37 shortwave transmitters of 500 kilowatts, compared to only 10 for the United States.

In 1982 RFE/RL transmitted an average of 816 hours per week while VOA transmitted 954, for a U.S. total of 1,770 hours.[3] The Soviet Union transmits a total of 2,100 hours per week, plus approximately 700 hours of "gray" transmissions, i.e., broadcasts that are not officially acknowledged. These gray stations are usually even more strident and often more effective than Radio Moscow. For example, the broadcasts of a "Radio Free Iran," ostensibly sponsored by a free Iranian revolutionary group within Iran, but actually originating from

Figure 2

HIGH POWER SHORTWAVE TRANSMITTERS
(200 Kw & Over)

	1961	1966	1972	1973	1974	1975	1976	1977	1978	1979	1980	1981
VOA	2	20	45	55	55	55	55	54	54	50	50	54
WORLD	16	51	185	221	244	255	350	373	369	370	383	408

Source: VOA Engineering Department; in *Voice of America Information Book*, Feburary 24, 1982.

Soviet territory, aired virulently anti-American messages before the overthrow of the Shah and during the hostage crisis.
The most glaring inadequacies of RFE/RL transmitting facilities are, surprisingly enough, those directed at the Soviet
Union. The transmissions to the European portions of the Russian Soviet Republic (i.e., west of the Urals) are subjected to
the most intensive jamming of all. Audience surveys indicate
that Radio Liberty broadcasts to this key region are listened
to by only about 6% of the population in an average week.
This is by far the lowest audience of any of RFE/RL broadcasts
to Europe, comparing, for example, with 26% in Czechoslovakia, 55% in Hungary, and 61% in Poland. The following
table lists the contrasts:[4]

*Percent of Population Listening At Least Once in Average
Week*

Russian Republic in Europe (except Moscow and Leningrad regions)	(3.5)
Moscow Region	7.6) Av. 6%
Leningrad Region	6.4)
Baltic Republics	10.1
Byelorussian Republic	13.0
Caucasian Republics	15.2
Central Asian Republics	4.9
Ukrainian Republic	10.8
Poland	61.3
Hungary	55.1
Rumania	55.0
Bulgaria	34.6
Czechoslovakia	26.0

These low figures may not be entirely due to transmission
and jamming problems. As described earlier, Radio Liberty
has had more difficulties than RFE in recent years with programming and management changes. Nevertheless, jamming
and inadequate transmitters appear to be the major problem.
The population in European Russia is the largest of any of

the Soviet bloc regions. From the point of view of political influence, it is also the most important. It represents the central focus of the Soviet ruling apparatus, a primary objective of any American effort at informing and influencing minds in the communist world.

There was not unanimous agreement in the RFE/RL community about proposals for increased transmitting power to European Russia. The BIB Annual report for 1982, for example, refers to a 1979 study which stated that the RL transmitting network by 1981 would be adequate to reach European Russia. The audience figures for 1982 seem to contradict this forecast, however. The new BIB management has placed new emphasis on increasing Radio Liberty's transmitting power to European Russia.

Another important area with inadequate coverage is Soviet Central Asia, where Radio Liberty reaches only about 4.9 percent of the population in an average week. Although RL does broadcast to this area in six languages (Russian, Uzbek, Kazakh, Kirghiz, Tajik, and Turkmen), the transmitters located in West Germany are too distant to be effective. No other Western broadcasts transmit to these areas in the local languages with the exception of VOA in Uzbek. Meanwhile, the political importance of this region has been growing steadily. A large majority of the population along the southern border is Moslem, and the people are highly aware of the political and religious turmoil in the independent Moslem countries to the south, including developments in Moslem Afghanistan. In addition, the population growth rates in these republics are much higher than those in the Great Russian regions of the Soviet Union, so that these areas should be of increasing importance in the future. The administration has focused on the need for new transmitters to beam adequate signals to these vast areas.

Both the BIB and VOA have requested supplemental budget amendments for fiscal year 1983, and increased capital budgets for subsequent years in order to finance improved transmission facilities. Plans are in progress for increased transmitter facilities in West Germany, the Iberian peninsula, the Middle East, and Asia.

Further steps to overcome jamming are also being considered. The U.S. delegation to the 1977 Belgrade conference on compliance with the Helsinki Accords on Security and Cooperation in Europe brought up the problem of jamming as a violation of this agreement. The nations of the European Community also expressed the view that jamming should be eliminated. Similar protests were made at the Madrid Conference in 1981, but jamming has continued unabated and has even increased in areas such as Poland.

There is a new U.S. interagency study group chaired by the Undersecretary of State for Security Assistance, Science and Technology, to examine the feasibility of launching direct broadcast satellites to relay American international broadcasts. Such a plan would pose many political, legal, and financial problems but is being considered as an effective way to reduce jamming.

National Security Decision Directive 77 signed by President Reagan on January 14, 1983 set up an International Broadcasting Committee, chaired by a representative of the National Security Council, to be responsible for the planning and coordination of the technical aspects of U.S. international broadcasting: "Among its principal responsibilities will be diplomatic and technical planning relative to modernization of U.S. international broadcasting capabilities, the development of anti-jamming strategies initiatives and techniques, planning relative to direct radio broadcasts by satellite and longer term considerations of the potential for direct T.V. broadcasting."

NOTES

1. Statement by Jozsef Takacs, Media Institute, op. cit., p. 24.
2. Report No. 97-480, 4/2/82, p. 3.
3. U.S. Information Agency, *Facts About VOA*, September 1982, p. 2; RFE/RL Inc. *Radio Free Europe/Radio Liberty—A Unique Broadcaster for 30 Years*, (Washington, 1982), p. 3.
4. RFE/RL: "Listening to Western Radio in East Europe, 1981-Early 82"; "Radio Liberty Listener Behavior Analysis, July-December 1981," Passim.

8
Personnel

There are four main categories of personnel in American broadcasting organizations: (1) *Media professionals* with backgrounds in private radio, TV, newspapers, or news services; (2) *Emigrés* or others with extensive backgrounds in foreign countries; (3) *Foreign Service Officers*; and (4) People appointed by the current administration, sometimes referred to as *"political appointees."* Differences in opinions and objectives among these four groups have been important factors contributing to disagreements over broadcasting policy in recent years. These groups can be described briefly as follows:

(1) *The media professionals* who make up most of the newsroom staffs of both organizations are primarily Americans in VOA but include several British Commonwealth citizens in RFE/RL. Most of the top executives of the Voice were professional broadcasters when it was launched in the 1940s. This tradition has continued in the newsroom, although many Directors of the Voice since World War II have had diverse backgrounds. In RFE, professional broadcasters were brought in soon

after its founding to provide more operational expertise in the Central Newsroom.

Many of the American newsmen in VOA, however, have had little international experience. Some of the criticism directed at VOA has been that its programming shows an excessive focus on news of interest to Americans, and less appreciation of issues which may interest foreign audiences. There are a number of examples: stories about the doings of middle level American officials of little interest to foreigners: a former governor of Illinois undergoing surgery for cancer, a Supreme Court Justice returning to duty after recovering from a stroke, a U.S. Senator who will not run again, or problems persuading pandas to mate in the Washington zoo. After the crash of an Air Florida jetliner in Washington in 1982, the Voice devoted several hours to a description of the crash and the rescue attempts. Although of major news value to Americans, one more accident of this type was of limited interest to foreign audiences in the opinion of many foreign-born journalists at VOA.[1]

One of the foreign language experts on the Voice calls this attitude "the Midwestern Syndrome," a failure to recognize that a topic of interest to middle America may not appeal to listeners abroad, especially those in communist countries hungry for news from the free world and listening to the Voice in spite of difficult jamming conditions, as well as the constant danger of being arrested.[2]

Another criticism directed at the Voice and RFE/RL newsrooms is that they have frequently gone too far in efforts to demonstrate "objectivity" by airing unfavorable news about life in the United States, in some cases even more extreme than the criticism appearing in domestic American media. This has been called by many the "warts and all" policy and is justified as a means of increasing believability. One foreign language desk expert has commented that the "Midwest Syndrome" in the newsroom has been replaced by a "Village Voice Syndrome." That is, younger recruits in the newsroom have ambitions to emulate their peers in the U.S. domestic media and become "investigative reporters" who will enhance their reputations by revealing scandals in American life. On the other hand, the professionals in the newsroom have been able to make substantial contributions by adding expertise in the editing of the news.

(2) *The emigrés* occupy most of the major positions in the various country and regional desks. These people, of course, have the most direct knowledge of conditions in their former homelands and ideas of how to appeal to their former fellow citizens. Many have been outstanding scholars or writers. Many members of the older generations witnessed the communist takeovers of their countries at first hand and saw relatives or friends killed or imprisoned and lose all their property during those days. The newer emigrés have lived under communist regimes for years. Most emigrés of all ages joined the U.S. broadcast agencies with a feeling of a mission, to assist their new homeland in the worldwide struggle against communism. In many cases they came up against what they considered to be a lack of understanding among so many Americans of communist aims at world domination, and the naiveté of many Americans in dealing with the Soviets.

With such large groups of people strongly committed to a cause, the management of the radio agencies has from the start felt the need for fastidious editing by the top executives. The trend towards greater executive oversight was accelerated after the Hungarian uprising of 1956, when RFE was widely accused of encouraging the idea that the United States would provide armed assistance to the freedom fighters. Editing became even more pronounced during the period of detente — "blanderizing," as it has been called by some critics. In RFE/RL, the country desks are governed by the news provided by the Central Newsroom. In addition there is a Broadcast Analysis Department, comprised of 37 people charged with checking all output of news and features for violations of the guidelines. This department issues a "Daily Broadcast Analysis," a 25 to 30 page report, which summarizes in English every feature and major news item of each language desk at considerable length. This report is reproduced and distributed daily throughout the organization.

In the Voice, up until 1982, the language desks were *required* to use the first ten news items produced regularly by the newsroom. This led the language services to complain that they were broadcasting large amounts of news with little appeal to their listeners.

The new management of the Voice moderated this policy in 1982. A menu of 14 to 15 news items is prepared by the newsroom, of which the language desks are *required* to broadcast three or four.

In regard to personnel policies, the emigrés in both agencies in recent years came to occupy a status somewhat inferior to Americans (or Commonwealth citizens in RFE/RL). In the Voice, this is partly a legal problem. Emigrés who are not citizens are in what is known as the GG category by the Civil Service and are not eligible for positions above the equivalent of the GS-12 level. Nor are they eligible for medical benefits or the federal retirement program.[3] But even emigrés who have lived in this country for decades and have become citizens have felt they were working at some disadvantage in recent years. This problem is more a matter of attitude by top management than a legal one. Since the Hungarian revolution, especially, management has feared that the foreign language personnel might be too "strident" if left uncontrolled. Contentions between the language experts and top management and the Central Newsroom increased and created significant friction. There are reports of the emigrés being referred to as the "freedom fighters," the "political exiles," or the "gypsies."[4]

The existence of Central Newsrooms that conduct most of the news decisions, the language desks' lack of scope for originating news items, and the excessive editing, combined to reduce the morale of the emigrés considerably. Many left in disillusionment. The feeling of inferior status was reinforced at VOA by the fact that personnel on the foreign language desks were usually receiving less pay than those on the worldwide english language desk performing equivalent duties.

Under the Reagan administration, the top management of VOA has been moving to correct many of these problems. The Voice now has its own Personnel Department for the first time, whereas previously it relied on USIA Personnel.

This new department has begun to take steps to correct the imbalance of pay scales between the English and foreign language desks. Emigrés are also being made eligible for medical benefits. VOA Personnel is also organizing a new Family Liaison Office to assist new emigrés adjusting to life in the United States.

The emigrés in Radio Free Europe/Radio Liberty are not particularly handicapped by legal restrictions, since it is a private corporation. But procedural problems do exist. Beginning with the 1956 Hungarian uprising, emigrés have generally been given less preference in promotions than the American or British Commonwealth news professionals and other American personnel. RFE/RL also suffers from problems of a wide range in pay scales due to its complicated history. At one time there were no less than seven scales. Radio Liberty brought others with it in the consolidation with RFE. There is one scale for American executive management, and another for American secretaries. German laws and union rules are strict and have resulted in additional scales. Management has now reduced the number to four and hopes to reach two scales eventually. These complications have generated morale problems, especially among foreign language personnel.

(3) *Foreign Service Officers*, the third group, includes Foreign Service Information Officers (FSIO) and Foreign Service Reserve (FSR). They serve officially only in VOA, but RFE/RL employs many Americans with equivalent backgrounds. Such people on the average have more experience in foreign countries than the professional newsmen. On the other hand, they tend to be more cautious than the emigrés and, like many in the Foreign Service, sometimes have a tendency to object to an activist broadcasting policy. It has been said that the diplomatic community as a whole distrusts the Voice and the Radios because they so often work at cross purposes with the diplomats. Foreign Service Officers generally deal with individual officials in foreign countries, and their main objective is to encourage friendly relations and accomplish specific foreign policy goals. The VOA and the Radios, on the other hand, appeal to large populations as a whole. Their mission is to de-

scribe American foreign policy, or to tell the truth about conditions in communist countries in clear and frank terms, or to provide accurate commentaries on the virtues of democracy and the shortcomings of communism. Inevitably, this mission often complicates the diplomat's efforts to promote more friendly relations with individual communist officials.

Some Foreign Service Officers who are serving a few years' tour of duty with VOA may bring these attitudes with them. Some may also be held back by the principle that you can get into trouble by doing something energetic, but you can't get into trouble by *not* doing something. They may be reluctant to promote an active policy if they fear such an initiative will cause them to receive future assignments in an undesirable post.

(4) *Administration Appointees.* These are people at the Voice appointed by the administration in power and are not career civil servants. The Director at present is in what is known as Executive Level 5 (part of a series of rankings from 1 to 5, 1 being the highest ranking given to such officials as Supreme Court Justices, Cabinet Secretaries, etc.). Next in line are a few other top officials in VOA with rankings equivalent to GS-16 or above who are classified as part of the "Non-career Senior Executive Service." All other people appointed by the administration at lower levels are classified as "Schedule C." Such people are presumed to be those primarily responsible for seeing that policy changes desired by any new administration are implemented. Up to the present there have been only a few such appointees in the Voice under the Reagan administration.

NOTES

1. Internal USICA memo, August 14, 1981.
2. Media Institute, op. cit., p. 26.
3. Interviews with VOA Personnel Department. GG is an old Civil Service term and the Personnel Department says that no one in

VOA or USIA Personnel knows what it stood for. GS means "General Schedule."

4. Interviews with foreign language desk writers, editors, and retirees. See also statement by Jozsef Takacs, Chief of Hungarian Service, VOA at Media Institute, op. cit., p. 22.

9

Programming

As outlined above, by 1980 the management and direction of American broadcasting organizations were largely against an activist broadcasting policy. The Reagan administration in 1981 pledged to a break with this trend. As Reagan said in the British Parliament, the objectives would be "to foster the infrastructure of democracy — the system of a free press, unions, political parties, universities — which allow a people to choose their own way, to develop their own culture, to reconcile their own differences through peaceful means."

These changes harked back to the programming policies of the years before 1964 when the VOA and the Radios had been making similar attempts to encourage the growth of free institutions in communist countries. These policies were articulated by the memo of C. Rodney Smith, Director of RFE, in 1963, and the handbook for the VOA in 1953, both quoted earlier.

In late 1980 and early 1981, similar memos were circulating among those in the foreign policy transition team, the State Department, and USICA who had responsibility for planning the information policies of the new administration. In addition to reviving some of the ideas used earlier in the 1950s and

1960s, a new set of proposals was emerging. The new theme that appeared in many of these memos and discussions was that American broadcasting and our information program in general should make a greater effort to stress the *values* of America and the democratic West. The aim was to find a more activist strategy that would not spawn unsupportable calls for uprisings.

Following are excerpts from one such memo prepared for the State Department transition team:

> *Problem:* People in VOA believe that the credibility of VOA should not be compromised by broadcasting anything that has the appearance of pro-American propaganda.

> *Response:* The credibility of VOA is indeed its most important asset. But broadcasting the *truth* about America and about other international events affecting American interests need not damage VOA's credibility at all.

> VOA's first mission should be to broadcast the truth and insofar as it does so its credibility will survive. Its second mission should be to broadcast the truth in ways that: (1) defend the U.S. against hostile propaganda and lies; (2) create sympathizers abroad; and (3) give audiences in other nations (and especially totalitarian nations) *a choice of political points of view.* Defense against hostile propaganda (especially by broadcasting corrections to lies and disinformation) is necessary if we want to prevent people from being manipulated into taking hostile actions against us.

> The creation of sympathizers abroad is necessary if we want to induce soldiers in enemy armies to have a "shaky" aim. To present foreigners with a choice of political points of view means essentially to introduce them to *American political philosophy.* They are already being bombarded with communist and other leftist propaganda; so the broadcast of another philosophy not only introduces them to that philosophy but exposes them to a situation of pluralistic choice — the very hallmark of the American system. All of these measures add up to an effort once again to win the hearts and minds of people to the cause of freedom and democracy. At a time when our relationship with the U.S.S.R. and its proxies is described as one of "cooperation and competition" it is time to use the VOA and ICA as tools in the competition.[1]

John Lenczowski makes similar points:

What is needed, literally is a new, yet traditional foreign policy 'doctrine,' with all the ideological connotations that the word inspires . . . . The centerpiece of such a doctrine must be those values which have made America a revolutionary political success . . . . America needs a campaign to reaffirm the goodness and essential justice of our system.[2]

A memo circulating in USICA applied these ideas directly to the Voice of America:

How and why VOA's mission was lost sight of.

The VOA's original prohibition against telling deliberate lies is now understood as a mandate to *report "balanced" and "objective" news.* The change is all-important. In fact, the word *truth* does *not even appear in VOA's Charter.*

The moral presuppositions of the Cold War were that the principles of the Communist movement were inherently tyrannical and constituted a threat to the security of free nations. The 1970s brought a major foreign policy change in the form of *detente.* The major premise underlying detente, however, was that the Soviet Union was not essentially different from other nations and would therefore behave normally if treated normally. To take this policy seriously one had to ignore that the Soviets were attempting to batten down on the rest of the world a tyranny like the one existing in Russia and were doing so in perfect accordance with their avowed principles. Detentist policy thus required that one be insensitive to the moral and political differences between the Soviet Union and other nations, and wary of, if not hostile to, those who insisted upon the reality of those differences. This politically inspired moral indifference leads to the spectacle of U.S. officials apologizing for and "covering" Soviet actions which undermined the assumptions of detente. It also meant that some things were simply not broadcast so as not to upset the Soviets. . . .

The detritus from the period of detente remains with us and is still deeply embedded in the policies of the bureaucracy.

The major effect of detente on VOA was to call into question its original raison d'etre, which was to tell the truth about the Soviet Union and the United States and thus to counter the defamations of Communist propaganda. Since VOA's very purpose was at odds with the premises of detente, it's hardly surprising that its sense of mission was badly damaged. . . .

A. Objectivity. The policy of moral neutrality enforced by detente took philosophical hold at VOA in the form of the misunderstood standards of "balance" and "objectivity." "Objectivity" in this sense has come to mean "value-free," *i.e.*, refusing to distinguish between good and evil and seeing in those terms nothing but subjective or personal preferences. Under the standard of value-free objectivity, one man's evaluation of American foreign policy, society, etc. must be as good as another's, and so, one man's view will be balanced against another's opposing view in VOA broadcasts in order to preserve "objectivity.[3]

One veteran journalist on one of the language desks at RFE in Munich provided this writer with a memo expressing similar ideas on the proper mission for the Radios' broadcasting to communist countries:

The Radios have operated for several years on the assumption that people behind the Iron Curtain are basically in agreement with Western values and that all we need to do is keep feeding them accurate *news* and they will make up their own minds in the right direction. But this is not the case. The peoples in these countries have been subjected to Communist propaganda from the cradle to the grave for a period that now spans a generation in Eastern Europe and two generations in the Soviet Union. The people have been so inundated that even when they reject their regime's line, they are still left without any foundation of their own and retain many attitudes foreign to western values. . . .

The Communist propaganda has a goal: to weaken our camp. We need a goal also. Our goal should be to weaken the Communist camp, not by stirring up revolts, but by giving the people alternative values that they can use in bringing about peaceful change. . . . At present all we are doing is informing, but what is the point of continually providing information without goals? What is the point of our broadcasting?[4]

After it took office in January 1981, the new administration moved to implement these recommendations for changes in information policy.

As one minor gesture, the name of the U.S. International Communications Agency was changed back to the former name, the U.S. Information Agency, as of August 1982, thus giving some hint that its mission would be directed more towards the former objectives of promoting American policies rather than promoting only two way "communications." USIA Director Charles Wick lauched "Project Truth," an extensive program to offset communist propaganda efforts around the world.

One major new proposal was for a special broadcasting service to Cuba, in effect a surrogate home service similar to those provided to Eastern Europe and the U.S.S.R. by RFE/RL. First called Radio Free Cuba, the service proposed was later dubbed Radio Marti.

In the Voice of America these new attempts by the administration to move beyond straight news and "objectivity" in programming met with some opposition from the Central Newsroom and many in management. In spite of new executive efforts, the attitudes resisting commentaries critical of communism continued. Examples include the following:

— At an early meeting of senior USICA management, Charles Wick suggested that Solzhenitsyn be invited to broadcast on the Voice. Wick was informed by the head of the Voice Russian Desk, an FSI officer with some experience in the Soviet Union, that Solzhenitsyn is considered a traitor by the majority of Soviet listeners, that he engages in an objectionable form of Soviet nationalism, that he is unpopular in Russia except with a small group of intellectuals, and should not be used on the Voice except as a "news" item. Subsequent checks with a broad spectrum of the Russian emigré community drew the conclusion that these statements were almost the opposite of the truth.[5] (Under new management some efforts are now being made to have Solzhenitsyn appear on the Voice.)

— When President Reagan announced his shortlived boycott of firms selling pipeline equipment to the Soviets, the Voice followed the announcement with the TASS dispatch coupled with dispatches from European services attacking the decision.

— The Voice gave air time to Georgi Arbatov, head of the Institute for the U.S.A. and Canada in Moscow, to criticize American defense policy. Arbatov's institute is in fact an organ of the Communist Party's Central Committee, which directs Soviet propaganda agencies on the best means for manipulating American public opinion and world opinion in regard to the United States. When the Director of the Voice complained to the news section about this decision and asked who was responsible, he was told the question amounted to "McCarthyism."

— On July 19, 1982, the President gave a speech in the Rose Garden on the occasion of signing the annual Captive Nations Proclamation. Reagan's 1981 proclamation had broken the trend of a steady softening in the language of this annual statement. Reagan's 1982 speech also contained activist rhetoric on the status of the "captive nations." As an indication of the contrary opinions among the Voice news staff, while this speech was coming in over the loudspeaker in the VOA newsroom in New York City, it was greeted by frequent groans and hisses by the newsmen present.[6]

— As late as September 1982, a Voice Latin American correspondent, Sean Kelly, interviewed Fidel Castro in Havana on the same day that the Senate Foreign Relations Committee was considering a bill to authorize Radio Marti. Castro attacked the idea and said that Cuba would probably retaliate in some way. Castro added that he did enjoy listening to the Voice of America and that he would prefer it to Radio Marti. This interview was broadcast over the Voice.

The old conflicts over whether or not to be governed by administration "policy," which had almost died out during the period when the former administrations and the Voice were following more pro-detente policies, came to the fore again, with the State Department and USIA insisting on more control over Voice output. The resulting contention spilled over into the media, with numerous leaks. The Voice had three Directors in the first 19 months of the Reagan Administration (James Conkling, John Hughes, Kenneth Tomlinson). Several members of senior management resigned. The third Director, Kenneth Tomlinson, formerly with the *Reader's Digest*, was appointed in the fall of 1982.

Meanwhile, further changes have been made in the senior management and policies. A new department has been formed to write commentaries, which delivers from five to seven items per week. The Policy Department has the authority to approve the commentaries provided for the U.S. foreign policy translators. It, in turn, is guided on policy by the USIA, which takes guidance on policy from the State Department. In practice there is a high degree of simultaneous communication between the policy representatives in all three organizations: VOA, USIA, and State. The Policy Department does not at this time exert any authority over the news programs.

Until late 1982, when organizational changes were made, the administration had similar difficulties in bringing about changes in the policies of RFE/RL. Since the Radios were governed by an independent corporation, they were not as subject to direct control by the administration or by the management of the BIB, which could only advise and monitor performance after the fact.

Meanwhile, the Radios continued to follow policies in line with principles that had been growing over the years since the Johnson administration, generally based on a high degree of "objectivity" and an avoidance of criticism of communism or the communist governments. The efforts at objectivity often resulted in portrayals that some critics contend succeeded in magnifying the "warts" in Western society beyond the needs of "objectivity." A few examples from recent years follow:

— In a effort to appear "modern" and appeal to the younger generation, the Hungarian service broadcast interviews with the madame of a leading sex establishment in Germany and with a transvestite actor/actress in Munich, programming that would not have been accepted by even the most avant-garde broadcasters in the United States.

— At the time of Reagan's inauguration, the Radios broadcast material more critical of the new administration than even the networks in the United States, which have been accused of having a "liberal" tilt. For example, the Radios aired frequent comments to the effect that "Hollywood was invading Washington," that Reagan was the "first actor" and "first divorced man" to be elected President, and that his administration was going to favor the rich over the poor. There was criticism of the twentieth amendment of the U.S. Constitution as being obsolete because of the "lame duck" lag between the election and inauguration day.

— At the time of the initial unrest in Poland in 1980 leading to the disturbances over the Solidarity trade union, top management at RFE was requiring such an "objective" tone that most news of the disturbances was being suppressed. Some members of the Polish language service insisted on a meeting with top management. The discussion became heated to an extraordinary degree before management agreed to allow more news of the unrest to be broadcast.[7]

To mitigate the policy-control conflicts, in late 1982 supervision by administration appointees was made more direct by the passage through Congress of the so-called Pell Amendment. This amendment to the original act setting up the BIB had been introduced first in the Senate in 1977 by Senators Claiborne Pell (D–R.I.) and Charles Percy (R–Ill.). It was designed to resolve the difficulties that had arisen since the formation of the BIB due to confused lines of authority between the BIB and the independent Board of Directors of RFE/RL. Attempts over the years to solve the problems of overlapping responsibilities and functions were generally unsuccessful, and so the tensions and controversies persisted.

The Pell Amendment in effect combined the two boards by specifying that the Board of Directors of RFE/RL Inc. would henceforth consist of the members of the BIB. The BIB was enlarged from five to nine voting members appointed by the President of the United States, plus the President of RFE/RL as a nonvoting member.

There have been many differences of opinion in the international broadcasting community about the wisdom of this step, which did in fact lessen the "independence" of the Radios. But there was no doubt that it did away with contention between the two boards and facilitated direction of the Radios by those appointed by the administration.

Frank Shakespeare, Chairman of the BIB, appointed former U.S. Senator James Buckley as the new President of RFE/RL. He named George Bailey to be Director of Radio Liberty, a post that had been open for two years to the detriment of the operations of that service. Bailey is a former executive editor of *Reporter* magazine and was an ABC News correspondent in Europe. He was a coordinating editor of *Kontinent*, a quarterly Russian language magazine published in Paris. Fluent in Russian, Bailey served during World War II as a liaison officer with the Red Army.

So three years after the start of the Reagan administration, new managements had been installed at both broadcasting organizations and new policies were beginning to be implemented. Presumably, these polices were more in line with the foreign policy of the administration.

NOTES

1. "The Mandate and Mission of the VOA and The ICA," Internal Memo, December 1980.
2. John Lenczowski, "A Foreign Policy for Reaganauts," *Policy Review*, Fall 1981, pp. 77–95.
3. Internal USICA memo, August 14, 1981.
4. Memo of 7/8/82. Writer preferred to remain anonymous.
5. Interviews with Dr. Igor Glagolev, formerly of the Soviet Academy of Sciences and advisor to the Soviet Salt I negotiating team, and Lev Navrozov, formerly a leading translator of English in the Soviet Union. This incident and canvass of Russian emigrés was also mentioned in the internal USICA memo of August 1981 on "The Voice of America" cited above.
6. Interviews with Voice foreign and news desk editors.
7. Interviews with RFE language and desk writers.

Part III
CONCLUSIONS AND RECOMMENDATIONS

10
Conclusions

After nearly half a century as part of the nation's security apparatus, radio still leads an uneasy life. It has had any number of homes, in the Office of War Information, the State Department, Defense Department, the Central Intelligence Agency, several versions of the United States Information Agency, and various private-citizen Boards. This frequency of reorganization testifies to the basic questions that keep coming up, getting answered, and then arising again: What is it? Who needs it? Why?

The most basic question — does radio belong in the national security system at all? — seems to have been settled. As the nation rushed from war to peace in 1945 and 1946, the Voice of America survived, but barely. Its fate hung in the balance as critics like Walter Lippman argued that broadcasting had no business as an arm of democratic government in peacetime. One can speculate on what would have happened to the VOA and its associated information programs had the Cold War not intruded.

As the historical record surveyed in these pages reveals, radio has risen and fallen in almost precise correlation with the tenor of conflict between the United States and the Soviet Union. At any point, it is possible to take the temperature of that conflict by examining the money, manpower and other resources allocated to the several radio services.

Thus, for example, 1947 to 1952 was a period of growth for the Voice, and of birth for Radio Free Europe, Radio Liberation and Radio in the American Sector, Berlin (RIAS). 1953 to 1961, by contrast, saw retrenchment and constriction of mission for all. Then, more ups and downs, followed by the present search for new guidelines — witness to the broader uncertainties about American foreign and defense policies, strategies, and tactics.

Two conclusions follow from this troubled record. First, radio has an indispensable role in national security. Whatever the misgivings, and however protracted the controversies may remain, strategic broadcasting is here to stay, at least as long as the struggle with adversary communism lasts. Put more crudely, America may not always understand or welcome its international broadcasters, but it is convinced it cannot do without them.

Second, with survival no longer the issue, the controversies have swirled around mission. Congress, provider of charters and funds, has its own ideas about information and broadcast objectives. Cabinet officers, sub-Cabinet and top-level bureaucrats have their views. So have the staffs of the radios, who have seen Directors come and go for a long time. As for the Directors themselves, they would come in with plans for change and improvement, usually with the imprimatur of the President, and find much of their energies taken up with their own survival.

No disparagement of the people involved is implied. Information, and radio in particular, is too new to American foreign policy to have generated any set of established principles. Information may have a charter, but it has no body of doctrine. What it does have is an array of debates which takes the place of dominant wisdom. The terms of those debates serve as the parameters within which the radios function, now tending toward one position, now toward the opposite. To recapitulate the principal issues identified in this survey:

* Persuading versus reporting.
* Selectivity versus objectivity.
* "Interesting" versus "important" program content.
* Two-way "communication" versus one-way "messaging."
* Western values versus life under communism in programming.
* Targeting communist elites versus populations as a whole.
* Conformity to U.S. policy versus criticism of policy.

At first glance, the range and depth of these controversies seem like a portrait of chaos; to those who have worked in and managed the radios, the feeling has been overwhelming at times. Without some such flexibility, however, it is doubtful that the radios would have survived, given the gyrations in foreign policy through the years.

There is, thus, a logic to the jumble of controversy, a logic of choice. On the record, the radios can be instruments of an activist foreign and defense policy, carrying the psychological offensive to the adversary. The restraints on the broadcasts from 1953 on, imposed from within and without, show how well this power is appreciated. That is one choice. The other is to make the radios the instrument of an accommodationist policy, as they were in the early part of the Carter administration and in the later 1950's.

The radios have been both, at different times, and can be either, now and in the future. But what has too often been ignored in the heat of debate is that the choices that must be made to begin with occur outside the Radios. The writers and the managers cannot — and, like the soldiers and the generals, should not try to — make the policy that guides them.

As with every enterprise, public or private, there is the test of effectiveness. Recommendations for improving effectiveness are always essential. But to argue about them is sterile without a clear answer to the question, "Effective for what?" Audience research estimate how many people listen, where and how frequently; alone it cannot judge whether the effects on their behavior are desirable or not. Historical and contemporary analysis of the radios must make its own choice if recommendations are to follow.

The conclusion of this study is that, on balance, the trend toward the activist role has prevailed over its opposite. The administration at the end of World War II had little enthusiasm for strategic radio in the period ahead. Yet, before it left office, not only had the wartime VOA been refurbished, but RIAS and the two Freedom Radios had been created.

This experience became the model for subsequent developments. Radio was downgraded more than once as hopes for detente rose. In at least one administration, Carter's, it was conceived as a contributor to detente through two-way dialogue. Neither deemphasis of radio nor reconstitution as a benign communication channel had much observable impact on the underlying conflict, and every diminution of radio's charter was followed by a reinvigoration. It may be confidently predicted that the activist model will govern for the foreseeable future.

The present is one of the times of reinvigoration, and for classic reasons. Foreign policy is patently more offense-minded than accommodationist. And while the incumbent administration adheres strictly to the established prohibition of incitement to open rebellion, the Radios are expected to serve much more actively.

There is no lack of recommendations for increasing effectiveness along those lines. The following sections present those on which there appears to be a consensus, and which are deemed most relevant.

11
Recommendations

PHYSICAL EQUIPMENT AND PERSONNEL

While there have been disagreements among those involved in broadcasting policy over programming and personnel matters, almost all parties agree that the transmission equipment of the Voice and the Radios is badly in need of replacement and expansion.

The areas to which transmission must be improved most urgently are European Russia, Poland, and the Moslem Republics of the U.S.S.R. The first two areas suffer from the most intensive jamming of all the RFE/RL target areas. The latter republics simply have been traditionally neglected by the shapers of American broadcasting policy.

As described in Chapter 7, the Radio Liberty audience coverage in European Russia and the Moslem Republics is the lowest of any areas reached by RFE/RL, only 6 percent and 4.9 percent respectively in an average week. Yet European Russia probably represents the most important single area reached by RFE/RL: the heart of the Soviet Union, with the largest cities and central governing bodies. For this reason, it is also subjected to the heaviest jamming by Soviet authorities. A major enhancement of present RL transmitting facilities is needed to overcome this jamming.

Poland also has been subjected to intense jamming since the birth of the Solidarity movement in 1980, most of which has originated from stations in the Soviet Union or Soviet jamming facilities moved into Poland. This mobile jamming poses a particular problem in that such "jammers" can be shifted to other Eastern European countries, according to need, and it suggests a need for RFE/RL transmitters that also can be shifted from one area to another as political and jamming situations dictate.

The issue of increasing the transmission facilities of both RFE/RL and VOA is now being studied, and the Reagan Administration appears determined to develop a coordinated, long range plan to ensure optimum use of the proposed transmitters. There is some agreement in Congress that funding for this expansion program will be approved pending the completion of such a plan.[1]

Such agreement on the need for better facilities to European Russia is recent. As late as 1980 the BIB was saying that existing transmitters for European Russia were adequate, but it now agrees that more facilities are needed. One problem is the location of the proposed additional transmitters and the available wavelengths. The best locations for transmitters are either Western Europe or the Near East. Western Europe already is highly congested, and in the Near East the problem is one of reaching an agreement with a country that could provide adequate security measures.

Additional transmitters are also badly needed to reach the Central Asian Republics of the U.S.S.R. where audience coverage is also low. As described earlier, these republics represent the fastest growing population areas of the Soviet Union, and are also politically and strategically important. Again, the primary problem is the emplacement of additional transmitters, which would also require a suitable host nation in the Middle East or South Asia.

The need for a major expansion and modernization of physical facilities was clearly demonstrated most recently in the aftermath of the shooting down of the Korean Airlines Flight 007, particularly in the case of the Voice of America. USIA mounted a major campaign to disseminate the news of this massacre to the people of the world. It soon became apparent from monitoring U.S.S.R. transmissions that the Soviets were not telling their people and those in their client countries that the plane had been shot down by a Soviet fighter. In fact, in Rumania there was no mention whatever of the incident for a full week. VOA devoted a major effort to airing the latest news about the shootdown and increased its broadcasting into the Soviet Union by 90 hours per day, attempting to avoid the heavy jamming by using multiple frequencies and by "surprise" schedules. But this effort required a heavy overload on the equipment, much of which had been scheduled for periodic maintenance, and the increased output could not be sustained beyond two weeks. VOA's problems in maintaining enhanced scheduling during the 007 situation was simply one more illustration of the inadequate facilities available to allow it to meet the requirements of an emergency.

RFE/RL also gave the KAL 007 story major emphasis. Since RFE/RL already broadcasts 24 hours a day to the Soviet Union and Warsaw Pact countries, this did not require any increased load on facilities, only concentrated emphasis on the news. Such details as the recordings of the Russian pilots' conversations with their ground control provided ideal material for RFE/RL broadcasts to areas with some familiarity with the Russian language. RFE/RL management is convinced that RFE/RL and VOA broadcasts into communist countries were a major factor in the eventual Soviet admission of their role in the incident.[2]

Meetings of the World Radio Administrative Conference are scheduled for 1984 and 1986, at which problems of available frequencies will be discussed. In view of the increasingly crowded state of the international airwaves, these meetings will be a major diplomatic undertaking for the United States, if it hopes to expand transmissions. For the longer term, studies are now being focused on the transmission of radio signals by direct broadcast satellites (DBS). Such a broadcasting mode would be highly effective in circumventing jamming efforts, but the many technical and political problems involved preclude a DBS system from becoming operationally feasible in the near future. Further studies are underway regarding the possibility of direct satellite transmission of television. This would provide broadcasting to communist countries that would have much greater impact than radio, but television also posits even greater technical and political quandries. For example, under present technology, television receivers would have to be dish antennas, which are now being bought by private owners in the United States, but are certainly not available to citizens of Soviet bloc nations.

PERSONNEL

The recommendations regarding personnel include the urgent need for more staff in the language services of both RFE/RL and VOA. In addition changes are needed in personnel policies at the Voice of America in terms of the role of Foreign Service Officers and the status of foreign-born personnel.

As described in Chapter 8, Foreign Service Officers (FSOs) had not been assigned to the Voice in the early days but began to be recruited by George Allen as a measure to increase cooperation between the Voice and the State Department. Few question that FSOs add national and regional expertise to the Voice, and assistance in implementing State Department policy. Objections come from both sides of the "objectivity" versus "policy" controversy. The "objectivity" partisans believe that FSOs wield excessive influence in passing along State Department policy. On the other hand, the "policy" advocates, who feel the Voice should be used as a more active arm of American foreign policy, complain that many Foreign Service Officers try to "blanderize" the Voice message.

The critics of Foreign Service Officers in broadcasting contend that the role of the FSOs in the Voice should be reduced if not eliminated entirely.[3] Certainly, the critics claim, they should not be placed in high-level positions determining major broadcasting policies. In most cases FSOs are on rotation so that they would only be in such positions for from two to four years. Such positions, it is argued, should be reserved for professional broadcasters, journalists, and foreign born experts who are devoting entire careers to international broadcasting and communications. Up until last year there were a number of Foreign Service Officers occupying high level posts in VOA, but almost all such positions are now held by professional journalists, broadcasters, or career VOA people.

The other major recommendation concerns foreign born personnel at the Voice of America. These people generally represent the most audience-knowledgable broadcasters at most of the language desks. They are in effect the actual "voice" of the Voice of America, except for the various English language services. Until 1981, however, they were working under several disadvantages. Now that the Voice has its own personnel department, some procedural improvements are underway, particularly in terms of medical and retirement benefits. But much still remains to be done. As of January 1983, new openings for "broadcasters" in the foreign language desks were still being ranked lower than equivalent openings for "broadcasters" in the English language services, although the former require skills in two languages.[4] Likewise, few of the new top positions in the new VOA administration were assigned to people from the foreign language services.

Recruiting and training of personnel for the foreign language services remains relatively weak. The new personnel department has done much to recruit top level executives and English language broadcasters from within the United States. But the hiring of foreign language experts is still lagging. It requires almost a year to get a recruit approved through the civil service and security clearance process, and many prospects give up and go elsewhere during that time.

Almost all of the language services in both the Voice and RFE/RL are seriously in need of additional personnel. Many of the language staffers at the Voice are overworked with multiple jobs such as translating, research, and rewriting. In Radio Liberty, for example, the nationalities desks urgently need more manpower. The three smallest (Tajik, Kirghiz, and Turkmen) have only five people each doing all the research, translating, and rewriting to produce daily programs. Allowing for sickness and vacations, some RL language desks are so shorthanded that enormous amounts of valuable material never get broadcast.[5] Such additional personnel are accounted for, in part, in the increased budgets recently requested for both services.

PROGRAMMING

Programming problems have arisen fundamentally from policy problems beyond the ability of the Radios to influence. As the nation itself has veered between great alarm over Soviet behavior and complacency that the Soviets were "mellowing," in Kennan's terms, the question of what the Radios were in business for could not be settled for any length of time. Broadcasting strategy can be no more surefooted than the national strategy it derives from.

Over the years since 1945, some policy ambiguities have been resolved. "Liberation" or "rollback" of communism via violent revolt is not an option. Whatever the Radios' mission, they are not calling for an uprising. But neither are they agents of acquiesence in the Soviet rule imposed on Eastern Europe. As the recent experience of the Carter administration demonstrated, two-way dialogue with the U.S.S.R. cannot mitigate significantly the systemic conflict between the two superpowers. The Radios are part of that conflict, their role vaguely defined as keeping alive heart-and-mind resistance to Soviet repression.

The recommendations for programming set forth in the following pages take as their premise this mission of keeping resistance alive. For purposes of contrast, there is a brief look at how programming is conceived when the policy emphasis tends toward the opposite role — downplaying of conflict and underlining of "detente."

PROGRAMMING FOR A POLICY OF DETENTE

If it is assumed that the Soviets have become more moderate and are willing to work for genuine peaceful coexistence with the West, broadcasting policy should remain substantially as it was during the period from 1965 up through 1980. There should be heavy emphasis on objectivity and the dissemination of news, with a minimum of editorializing. The broadcasts would mute criticisms of the communist system, as this might cause undue tension with the communist authorities. For the Voice, there should be concentration on news of the United States and descriptions of American life, as well as international news as seen from an American point of view. The guideline should be, in President Carter's words: "Only by knowing and understanding each other's experiences can we find common ground on which we can examine and resolve our differences." Emphasis should be on exchange and the creation of mutual understanding.

Similarly, for RFE/RL, emphasis should be placed on news of primary interest to the peoples of Eastern Europe and the Soviet Union. There should be features and commentary on life in these countries but an avoidance of strong criticisms of the communist system, which, again, might lead to ill feelings by the leaders of these countries and increased tensions with the United States.

The Policy Guidelines for RFE/RL published in the 1978 annual report are clear: there should be "avoidance of sweeping generalizations, propagandistic argumentation, gratuitous value judgements, unsupported criticism of the communist system or its representatives, as well as the use of obsolete terminology such as 'The Communist bloc,' 'Communist satellite countries,' and 'Capitalism vs. Communism.'" Or to quote again the statement by the head of the RFE Hungarian Desk in an interview in the *N.Y. Times* in 1972: "We are not asking the Communists to give up Communism. . . . I am not entitled by the Hungarian people to represent or lead them. . . . We have to be realistic."

PROGRAMMING FOR A POLICY OF RESISTANCE

When U.S. foreign policy assumes that the Soviets and their allies continue to harbor aggressive designs, programming should be governed by policies that help to counter these ambitions. Broadcasting to the communist countries will be intended to weaken the Soviet capabilities to continue expansionist policies abroad. Program policies will resemble those of the period from 1957 through 1963, when the objective was to counter communist expansionism and to support peaceful reform of the central controls of the communist countries.

The Reagan administration has similar assumptions behind its foreign policy, as outlined earlier. Reagan has articulated the goal of encouraging the peaceful spread of democracy around the world, including the communist countries. Following up on his June 1982 speech before the British Parliament quoted earlier, the State Department arranged a Conference on the Democratization of Communist Countries in October 1982 in Washington. Secretary of State Shultz keynoted this meeting with a speech that included the following statements:

> In the final analysis, internal forces must be the major factors for democratization of Communist states. We do not seek to foment unrest or undermine Communist regimes. Yet we will not ignore the individuals and groups in Communist countries who seek peaceful change. It is our responsiblity, both moral and strategic, to meet their calls for help. We must aid their struggle for freedom. . . .
>
> The U.S. Government is active on this front:
>
> — Our radio broadcasts serve as the communist world's surrogate free press.
> — We are encouraging private sector groups to aid the peaceful struggle from freedom in Communist countries. . . .
>
> Some of you here today are political activists from Communist countries; advocates of freedom in your homelands. I believe that history will judge you as the apostles of hope; the forebears of a new age of democracy. We are committed to help you and your countrymen make the dream of freedom a reality.

These remarks indicate how important the Reagan administration considers American broadcasting as an element of this policy. Representatives of RFE/RL attended the conference, as did officials from USIA and the Voice.

Shultz returned to this theme in his statement on U.S.-Soviet relations before the Senate Foreign Relations Committee on June 15, 1983: "Not all the many external and internal factors affecting Soviet behaviour can be influenced by us. But we take it as part of our obligation to peace to encourage the gradual evolution of the Soviet system towards a more pluralistic political and economic system. . . ."[6]

Assuming that the above remarks represent the true parameters of the Reagan administration's policy towards the communist countries, what should its broadcasting policy be? If the 1957-63 period most closely parallels the administration's foreign policy and the attendant broadcasting objectives, what were the details of the broadcasting policies that would be applicable today and what additions might be considered?

It is first necessary to consider the enormity of the present propaganda effort conducted by the Soviets in the U.S.S.R. and in Eastern Europe. In spite of their homilies about the "Spirit of Helsinki," the Soviets consistently and virulently attack the United States and other Western democracies in internal broadcasts. A VOA language desk editor who emigrated from Eastern Europe after World War II recently returned from a visit to two Warsaw Pact countries. He reported that the volume of Radio Moscow and other Soviet propaganda has reached an unprecedented level, and that the constant barrage has had some effect, in spite of the general dislike of the Soviet Union. At a minimum, Soviet propagandists are succeeding in creating the impression that the United States is at least as much at fault as the U.S.S.R. in increasing global tensions.[7]

U.S. information programs that attempt to counter this propaganda with the message of American aims and Western ideals must take this huge Soviet program into account, not only in its size and scope, but also in terms of its subtleties and successes.

If the United States is trying to convince the people of the Soviet bloc that the Western democracies are striving for meaningful steps toward disarmament, and if we aim to encourage nonviolent reform processes in the East, then it is not sufficient merely to transmit objective news about current events and descriptions of life in America.

THE VOICE OF AMERICA

First, in regard to the Voice, treatment of news and commentaries should return more to the objectives defined in the earliest postwar mission statements: (1) to counter Soviet efforts to discredit the United States around the world, and (2) reach the people of the communist countries whom the communists were trying to cut off from all western information.

The Voice Charter, drawn up in 1959, has been frequently cited since then by those opposing any function for the Voice except the broadcasting of news and Americana. In fact, however, the wording of the Charter does not preclude an effort to offset Soviet anti-American propaganda. The second and third "principles" read: "2 — VOA will represent America, not any single segment of American society, and will therefore present a balanced and comprehensive projection of *significant American thought and institutions. 3 — VOA will present the policies of the United States clearly and effectively*, and will also present responsible discussion and opinion on these policies." (Emphasis added.)

These provisions would allow the Voice to mount an active campaign of refuting Soviet efforts to discredit the United States and to transmit the message to people behind the Iron Curtain about significant American thought and institutions as well as the policies of the United States and discussion of these policies. According to the latest audience estimates, nearly 50% of the Voice audience is in the Soviet Union or Eastern Europe—50 million out of a total audience of 103 million. This is another indication of the importance of taking Soviet propaganda into account when forming VOA programming policy. (Another 17%, or 18 million, are in mainland China, which means that nearly two thirds of all VOA listeners live under some form of communism.)[8]

Project Truth, launched by USIA in September 1981, does in fact include an effort to identify and counteract communist disinformation and has begun to use the commentaries on the Voice for this purpose. This initiative would seem to fall within the definition of a "projection of significant American thought and institutions" and "a presentation of the policies of the United States."

There has been contention over the degree to which the Voice should broadcast the opinions of those opposed to U.S. policies. In light of the Charter and the objectives of American foreign policy, it would seem that the soundest principles to govern this problem could be expressed in two parts: (1) comments by authoritative Americans, pro and con, on American policies might be broadcast; and (2), there is no need to give Voice air time to fringe groups or communist officials opposing American policies.

As specific examples, the Voice recently was subjected to criticism for broadcasting a statement by Lane Kirkland, President of the AFL/CIO, criticizing the administration's economic policies. This was an effort to convey an important segment of opinion in the United States, since the AFL/CIO represents a large consituency. Broadcasting Kirkland's comments also has the effect of demonstrating the independence of labor unions in this country.

On the other hand, Voice broadcasts of a talk by Georgi Arbatov and an interview with Fidel Castro, both attacking American foreign policies, raise serious questions. If American foreign policy assumes that the Soviets and their allies aim to overthrow the democratic West and expand communist influence by every possible means, there would appear to be little reason to give their spokesmen facilities on our own media to further their cause. Voice broadcasts of such figures could well confuse Voice listeners as to what American policy really is and our steadfastness in following that policy.

Along the same lines, the Charter would not appear to inhibit the Voice from broadcasting extensive commentaries promoting the *values* of Western civilization. As outlined above, the Voice in recent years has come under some criticism for allowing "objectivity" to become an excuse for "value free" communication. But the provision in the Charter calling for the "projection of American thought and institutions" certainly covers the subject of the background of American democracy. What is more, this heritage is by no means based entirely on *American* writers and statesmen. Much of our heritage is derived from the thinkers and writers of the past, as, for example, the thought of classical Greece and Rome, the statesmen of the Dutch Republic, and thinkers like John Locke and John Stuart Mill. This heritage could be aired as part of the commentaries without violating the Charter and could provide listeners in Soviet bloc areas and elsewhere with a set of values to compare with those being promoted by the communist propaganda apparatus.

Such policies would not need to violate the Voice's mission to provide accurate and objective news. The contention that erupted in the Voice in 1981 over "news" versus "propaganda," which spilled over into the media, seems in hindsight to have been exaggerated. The administration spokesmen were not recommending that the news output be distorted to favor American policy. They were objecting to the many examples of news output that appeared to feature American "warts" excessively, even more so than leading private American media. They were also advocating more commentaries explaining American policy and fewer features on aspects of American life that are of little interest to foreigners. None of these recommendations need violate the charter.

THE RADIOS

Since Radio Free Europe and Radio Liberty serve as surrogate home services, their problems are somewhat different from VOA's. They need to transmit the news of their target countries in a more comprehensive manner, since much vital information cannot be obtained from the local government-controlled media. They should also provide commentaries and features of a freer style than are available locally.

Even under an information program dedicated to the dissemination of the ideals of democracy, it is essential that the Radios continue to maintain a high degree of accuracy in the news accounts. Veracity has remained a paramount American policy at both the Voice and the Radios, since inaccuracy is the nemesis of credibility.

The features and the commentaries would appear to be the appropriate vehicles to transmit the messages of Western values to the peoples of the communist countries. From 1957 up through 1965, when this was the policy of the Radios, there was also a conscious effort to avoid stridency and polemics in the commentaries. Prudent and measured commentary is just as important today. And yet effective presentation of Western values can still be couched in reasonable terms.

From the late 1960s up until recently, the Radios, like the Voice, operated on the assumption that it was not too important to promote actively Western values to their audiences. It was believed that the people behind the Iron Curtain are basically in agreement with Western values, and that the primary responsibility of the Radios was to provide them with accurate *news*. Many in the language desks at the Radios and several other authorities were arguing that such is not the case, and more weight should be given to their reasons. The people in these countries, the argument goes, have been so inundated with Marxist-Leninist propaganda that even when they come to reject the regime's line, they still hold many attitudes foreign to Western values. For example, there is the Western concept of respect for diverse points of view. One Russian emigré, who defected to the West in 1969, said in a lecture on Radio Liberty that one of the most moving changes in his own thinking occurred when he read John Stuart Mill for the first time, especially Mill's description of the concept of respect for other, and perhaps contrary, opinions. This, said the emigré, is contrary to all doctrine in Soviet schools, where the students are taught to discriminate between "us" and "them," friends and enemies, heroes and villains. Anyone who is not for us is against us. The word *vrag* or "enemy" is a frequently used word in the Soviet vocabulary. *Klassovy vrag* is a class enemy, and *Glavny vrag* is the main enemy, or the United States.

Mikhail Borodin, the Soviet agent who was Stalin's representative with the Nationalist Chinese during their period of cooperation with the Soviets in the 1920s, once told the young Miss Soong (later to become Madame Chiang Kai-Shek) that the Western doctrine posing the most serious danger to communism was the Christian concept of *forgiveness*. This is the greatest threat to the Leninist *weltanschauung* of the class struggle and class enemies.[9]

The Radios could do much to provide an alternative set of values for people raised on such a propaganda diet, many of whom reject these Soviet teachings but are groping for other ideals. These values would include not only concepts of toleration and forgiveness, but all the other aspects of the Western democratic heritage built up over centuries of trial and error. This heritage encompasses not simply parliamentary democracy, but other tenets as well, such as freedom of worship, freedom of the press, freedom of speech, respect for the individual, freedom of emigration, and so on. All those issues have been touched upon from time to time by the Radios, but not in recent years as part of a unified effort to inform listeners in the Soviet bloc about an alternative belief system.[10]

Communism may be discredited among the large majority of people in communist countries as a political and economic framework, even among the elites, but many important remnants of the theory still dominate their thinking habits in the absence of other ideals. Communism still provides their standards for deciding whether people are "deviationists," and for dividing people into friends versus enemies. History is still considered to be determined by economics and the class struggle. State planning is still believed by many to be superior to a free economy, in spite of the failures of communist economic performance.[11]

If the United States is pursuing promotion of a gradual, peaceful democratization of communist countries, the Radios can be important in helping to fractionate and gradually dissipate central controls. The message would not call for armed uprisings but steadily encourage actions by the people to lobby for internal reform. The growth of the labor union movement in Poland is just one example of such a development, one that was aided by the free flow of information provided by RFE and other Western broadcasts.

The encouragement of peaceful change was an explicit policy of RFE in the early 1960s, as summarized in the memo from the Director, C. Rodney Smith, quoted earlier. Conditions in the communist countries have changed since 1963. Some of the objectives in the Smith memo are not as cogent now, but others are even more applicable. The following would be programming recommendations for RFE/RL at present:

(1) The lack of an efficient agricultural system in the Soviet bloc should be highlighted. The last decade has once again demonstrated the inadequacy of communist agricultural planning. Soviet agriculture continues to suffer in terms of productivity. The small percentage of land being tilled as private plots produces almost as much food as all the collectivized farms combined.

On the other hand, Solzhenitsyn and others have stated that the Soviet people have no knowledge of conditions on the farms, and even the collective farmers are unaware of the situation in other areas of the country. But all are thirsting for more knowledge of such conditions and explanations for their food problems. Anything more that can be done by the Radios to pressure the governments to enlarge the proportion of land being farmed by private farmers will contribute to the overall objective of shifting power from the central government to the people.

(2) Some broadcasts should aim to persuade the communist elites that *centralized management of industry* is an increasing obstacle to high rates of economic growth, that more local incentives and decentralized decision making are required. All the communist countries have recorded failures in their industrial plans. Those countries that have experimented with more decentralization, such as Yugoslavia and Hungary, have done better. As with agriculture, anything the Radios can do to stimulate decentralized industrial management serves to reinforce reformist sentiment in Eastern Europe and the U.S.S.R.

(3) Programs should support writers and artists in their struggle to liberate themselves from the cultural orthodoxy of socialist realism. Since 1963, as a result of spasmodic thaws in communist countries, there has been a periodic flowering of literature, art, and music. Outside Russia there has been a re-

discovery of the great poets of Russian literature of the earlier 20th century, who had been suppressed during Stalin's time but are now being resurrected in the West and broadcast to Soviet audiences. A similar galaxy of postwar writers has appeared in the underground *samizdat* or *tamizdat* publications, of whom Solzhenitsyn is only the most notable, whose work should be relayed to East bloc listeners.

(4) Similarly, *music*, both popular and classical, can be another major area for appealing to peoples in the communist countries, from several points of view.

In the classical field, the emigré communities from the Soviet Union and Eastern Europe in the West now include a large number of outstanding musicians. Their work has been used in Western broadcasts but could probably be used on a more systematic basis, through performances and discussions of modern music, much of which is discouraged in the Soviet Union. As one Russian emigré musician said, "If people are shown that it is possible to experiment with new ideas in music, it may also be possible to experiment with new ideas in economics and politics."[12]

American popular music has always been a major staple of VOA and the Radios, but there is evidence that it is no longer a unique feature for demonstrating the values of Western freedom to Iron Curtain young people. For many years the communist regimes tried to discourage Western jazz as decadent, but in an unintended tribute to the force of Western transmissions, they have long since abandoned this effort. In fact, communist stations now broadcast new Western popular releases as often as our radios do, and in some cases they receive new hits on the air *before* our stations do. There is some belief that the Radios are now overdoing the broadcasts of Western popular music, which, to many, no longer conveys the virtues of a free society.[13]

(5) In the past two decades there has been a great revival of *religious* beliefs within the communist countries. In Poland, of course, Catholicism was always the dominant force in society. But in the other Warsaw Pact countries, as the popu-

lations have become increasingly disillusioned with communism, they have been turning to religion. The governments themselves are worried about the growth of "believers" and spend a large amount of their own propaganda budgets attacking the problem. For example, among the total of 1.5 million full time propagandists in the Soviet Union, there are no less than 70,000 "atheist lecturers," devoting themselves to combatting religion.[14] The Russian Orthodox Church is permitted to function under severe restrictions as to the number of services, churches in operation, proselytization, religious education, and so on. Certain elements of the KGB are assigned from time to time to disrupt and disperse religious gatherings. Bibles are difficult to obtain. There are strong religious movements among laymen in communist bloc churches because of the fact that the clergy has been so heavily infiltrated or inhibited. Such lay movements could be encouraged.

In recent years the quality of Radio Liberty's religious broadcasts has deteriorated, according to some critics. Increased resources would allow it to raise its religious broadcasting back up to the standards it used to maintain when it was a separate identity.[15]

RFE broadcasts religious services regularly to the Eastern European countries, but increased budgets would allow an increase in religious programming. Anything that can be done to nurture religion in these communist countries could promote the growth of groups that would work within their countries against militarism and for a relaxation of controls.

(6) *Scientists.* Some broadcasts could be designed to appeal to a more limited, sophisticated audience such as scientists. Many in these groups are disillusioned with communist theory and yearn for philosophical and intellectual alternatives. They undoubtedly would welcome more enlightened discussions of scientific, philosophical, and theological issues.

There are many other subjects that broadcasts to Soviet scientists could cover that would in their own way spread Western values and bring into question the central authority of the Soviet state. For instance, programs could illustrate the importance of scientific and academic freedom in the West. Details could be provided on the overwhelming share of Soviet research being devoted to military-related efforts. Western scientists could be quoted, such as those who say that Soviet research historically has produced little in chemicals, pharmaceuticals, electronics and other technical products for civilian use.[16]

Another broadcast topic could be the coercion of scientists to manipulate their results in order to satisfy the government. A case in point is the psychiatric profession, which has been enlisted by the Soviet government to attack the dissident movement. Many dissidents are examined by psychiatrists, declared to be "schizophrenic," and frequently institutionalized, and subjected to brutal treatment with drugs. An American psychiatrist visiting the Soviet Union adds that some of the Russian doctors may be quite sincere. They may be making such diagnoses simply because their Soviet education and training cause them to believe that anyone opposing the system must be mentally ill.[17] American broadcasts would be beneficial in exposing Soviet scientists to Western principles of scientific inquiry, which refute and reject Soviet principles.

Broadcasts directed to the general public in the communist countries describing such practices would also be of value in informing the public about the true characteristics of their governments. Many people may not be aware of the unscientific nature of such practices.

The foregoing recommendations have stressed more programming to specific groups in the communist countries. RIAS was the first international broadcasting organization to find this method effective. RIAS developed special programs designed to appeal to farmers, labor union members, young people, and others in East Germany. RFE also instituted targeted programming in the 1960s. The Radios can and should increase the volume of broadcasts directed at specific groups. The following is a list of the further potentialities:

Farmers. Agriculture accounts for a much larger percentage of the work force in the communist countries than in the United States. These figures show how much larger:

Percent of Labor Force in Agriculture[18]

U.S.S.R.	26.0
Bulgaria	46.6
Czechoslovakia	16.9
Hungary	25.0
Poland	39.0
Rumania	56.0
Yugoslavia	49.8
U.S.A.	5.0

The audience research departments of RFE/RL do not separate farmers from other workers in their surveys. They are
all combined under the term "blue collar," so data on the size
and reactions of farmers in communist countries are not available. But these groups represent large potential audiences for
American broadcasts describing new farming techniques as
well as key information conveying the values of independent
agricultural enterprise in contrast to large government-controlled cooperatives.

Factory Managers and Industrial Executives. This group
should be open to the proposition that centralized planning is
not working. They see the results at first hand. In the Soviet
Union, factory managers as such have little independent responsibility. They are controlled almost completely by the central bureaucracy or by the Communist Party officials,
propaganda agents, and labor union bosses at the regional and
local level. Nevertheless, the elite groups in the industrial bur-
eaucracies should represent a sympathetic audience for more
information on both the flaws in the present system and the
advantages of more decentralization.

Youth. Young people are a tremendous, restless audience
for more outside information. As mentioned above, popular
music is no longer an exclusive attraction on Western radio,
since the East bloc radios have incorporated such music into
their broadcasts. More specialized programs covering the

problems young people face in communist countries are required. Project Truth is making a special effort to reach "the successor generation," or young people who will eventually occupy leadership positions in the U.S.S.R. and Eastern Europe.

Since the rise of Solidarity in Poland, the Communist Party has lost 800,000 members, and only 7,000 new members have joined, almost entirely young people.[19] All the nations require the continuing support of the younger generations to survive. Broadcasts directed towards the youth in Soviet bloc countries can help to diminish their likelihood of supporting communist governments in the future. It has been suggested that such programs could include descriptions of the opportunities for young people in the democracies: freer choice of education, job opportunities, voluntary military service, and other contrasts to conditions behind the Iron Curtain. Soviet authorities already have expressed concerned about growing resistance to military service among their young people. Such programs demand specialized work by writers and researchers, and should be an important priority for any increase in staff budgets at RFE/RL.

Women. It is a cliché of Marxist thought that women are the victims of discrimination under capitalism and will only attain true equality under communism. But in the Soviet Union and Eastern Europe women appear to be suffering sexual discrimination to a greater extent than women in the West. There is further evidence that the communist measures to loosen the rules about marriage and family ties have hurt women more than men, with the men finding it easier to get divorces and readjust later in life.[20]

RFE/RL has had no women's programs for several years, mainly because of budget constraints. These programs in past years attracted rather small audiences. This may have been because of their content rather than lack of interest among Eastern European women for Western broadcasts in general, since the audiences of both Radios have always included a large proportion of women (about 40 percent for Radio Liberty and 45 percent for RFE).[21]

Programs for women would seem to be an important area for further development when budgets are increased. Among other subjects, these programs could cover the progress in women's rights in the West as well as appealing to women's interests in the arts, music, religion, and family relations.

Ethnic Minorities. Within the U.S.S.R., such demographic groups should be high-priority target audiences. In 1979 Great Russians accounted for only 52.4 percent of the population of the Soviet Union. By the year 2000 many demographers expect this percentage to drop below 50 percent. The populations of the Central Asian Republics (Kazakhstan, Uzbekistan, Tajikstan, Turkmenistan, Kirghizia) are experiencing particularly high growth rates. In spite of official Soviet efforts to suppress emergent ethnic and national awareness in Central Asia, the Ukraine, and elsewhere, nationalist sentiment appears to be growing in the non-Russian areas of the U.S.S.R. The Ukrainians have always resented Russian rule, and the Byelorussians have been historically concerned about domination by the Great Russians.[22] The three Baltic Republics (Lithuania, Latvia, Estonia) were seized by the Soviets during World War II and their well established democratic governments and religious centers were crushed. They have been centers of repressed opposition ever since.

Radio Liberty now broadcasts to the non-Russian republics in fifteen languages, including Russian, more than any other Western radio. To many areas, however, RL broadcasts only one or two hours daily. Furthermore, as outlined in the section on Physical Equipment, the signals to the Central Asian Republics are weak. A top priority in any enhancement of Radio Liberty should be to add to the transmitting facilities directed to Central Asia, and to bolster the Central Asian programming staffs.

While the programs should not, of course, incite armed uprisings or active civil disobedience, they can do more to encourage pressure for greater decentralization and local autonomy. Programs should provide detailed treatments of the histories of these republics and place greater emphasis on world events that relate to decolonialization and the rights of smaller nations to self-determination.

Armed Services. Solzhenitsyn has often noted that the soldiers in the Soviet Union lead such spartan lives that they are pitied even by the downtrodden civilians. These soldiers and the sailors represent another major special interest group to be appealed to by our radios, not only to the Soviet Union but to the other Eastern European countries and to Cuba.

Soviet World Outlook, a monthly survey of the Soviet Press, writes: "The Soviet Armed Forces are suffering from a series of 'epidemics' such as infectious intestinal disorders, dysentery and hepatitis, according to an editorial in the May 1982 issue of the *Soviet Military-Medical Journal.* The diseases are said to be related to poor living conditions — overcrowded, dirty barracks, lack of sewage and garbage disposal systems, contaminated water supply — inadequate storage and handling of food, and poor personal hygiene. It is explicitly indicated that the problem is endemic and widespread throughout the Soviet Armed Forces, affecting combat readiness and morale."[23]

Many other appeals to these troops are possible. Why does the Soviet Union continue to keep so many men under arms? Why are no soldiers below the rank of colonel allowed to carry loaded arms, except under special conditions? A priority enhancement should be a special service of Radio Liberty to the Group of Soviet Forces, Germany. The Soviet Union already has a broadcasting service for this purpose, Radio Volga. Radio Liberty could mount an effective counter to this Soviet effort. Likewise, Radio Liberty could consider a special service for the Soviet troops in Afghanistan. This would be feasible only after transmission facilities are expanded enough to achieve adequate signals to Central Asia.

Similarly, when Radio Marti is organized, its directors should consider a special service for Cuban troops stationed in Africa. These men must represent an extremely receptive audience for free broadcasts. Why have they been sent to faraway lands where in many cases they face hostile local populations? Why are their wounded being sent to Eastern European hospitals rather than back to Cuba? Any weakening within these Cuban forces would be a setback for the Soviets.

There are many opportunities for broadcasting information

to the soldiers of the Eastern European countries that could be extremely valuable in reducing the abilities of Warsaw Pact forces to support the aggressive plans of the Soviet Union. In a recent interview, the following observations came from a man who recently emigrated from Poland and who held a senior position in which he was kept informed of Soviet strategy as it relates to the Polish Army:

Only the very top generals in the Polish Army and a few senior officials in Poland are aware of Soviet contingency plans for the invasion of Western Europe and how the Polish Army fits into these plans. Many in the West assume that the Polish Army would refuse to fight against NATO in such an eventuality, but that may not necessarily be the case. Firstly, Polish soldiers are kept virtually ignorant of politico-military developments. Secondly, the average Pole still hates the Germans as much as the Russians as a result of the bitter memories of World War II. If the Polish Army were caught up in a large scale invasion of West Germany, it is not clear at present whether anyone could or would organize a movement to resist such orders. Simple momentum might carry them along with the invasion.

The Polish Army is highly trained and the third largest in Europe, with 15 divisions and 400,000 men. The Soviet plans for a possible invasion of Western Europe call for a first wave of Soviet and East German troops to invade northern West Germany across the Fulda Gap, the north German plains, in order to break the West Germany Army. The U.S. Army now opposite Czechoslovakia will not be attacked unless or until it moves north. After this presumed breakthrough, the entire Polish Army will then be thrown into the second wave of the attack along with additional Soviet troops and will be directed to occupy Denmark and part of northern West Germany. The Polish Army will, therefore, be "used up" in a few days with little or no reserve. The campaign will be a blitzkrieg in which the Polish troops are not supposed to pause, even to attend to casualties. They will have been issued ammunition for only two days of fighting. There are ammunition dumps in East Germany that are to be used for resupply during the invasion. They will be followed by a third echelon of the Soviet forces assigned to occupy the conquered territories of Western Europe.[24]

According to the Polish emigré, only a handful of top Polish Communist Party officials and generals know of these plans, the implications of which are that if they are not immediately successful, the entire Polish Army will be virtually destroyed. In any event, Poland will be denuded of its own troops.

If these war plans could be conveyed to the Polish soldiers by western broadcasts, it would have appreciable effects on Army morale. It is difficult to reach soldiers in the Warsaw Pact countries since their access to radio is severely controlled. But descriptions of these war plans could be broadcast to Polish civilians in general, and the word eventually would spread rapidly to the Army, first through new conscripts and then through men returning from leave.

Such an information campaign might do much to undermine the reliability of the Polish Army, at least in the minds of Soviet military planners. Even if the Soviets begin to *think* that the Polish Army, with its 15 divisions, is unreliable, the perception would certainly complicate Soviet strategy. This is just one example of possible uses that might be made of broadcasts directed towards the armed forces in communist countries.

Reaching soldiers in the communist countries directly requires special methods to overcome the severe restrictions on listening in the armed services. But the problems are not insuperable. A clandestine Afghan radio service is reaching Soviet troops in Afghanistan now by broadcasting on a band that penetrates the garrison-wired radio system.[25] Additional budget allocations are also required to cover the costs of personnel and research necessary to do the specialized broadcasts.

General Programming. An important field of interest to all groups that should receive more attention by RFE/RL is *history*. Experts like Solzhenitsyn, as well as ordinary citizens surveyed by RFE/RL audience research have often stressed that the Radios should broadcast more programs on the history of these countries.[26] The communist governments have done their best to distort and alter the histories of Russia and Eastern Europe, in particular stories of brave and usually short attempts to develop truly democratic governments. In almost every Eastern European country, there were interludes when representative government held sway. Political parties emerged, proposed platforms, and had some chance to operate under parliamentary conditions. In the Soviet Union this process, unstable as it was, lasted only a short while between March and November of 1917 before the Bolshevik seizure of power. There are dramatic stories of the courageous and able individuals who led these parties, most of whom either had to flee for their lives, were assassinated, executed, or died in prison. These include Kerensky and his associates in Russia in 1917, almost the entire Free Polish Government, who were arrested and imprisoned in 1946 when they travelled to Moscow to negotiate, Ian Masaryk of Czechoslovakia, who was murdered during the communist takeover of Prague, Imre Nagy in Hungary, and Iuliu Maniu of Rumania, leader of the Farmer Labor Party. Maniu was considered potentially Rumania's greatest democratic statesman. He participated in a short-lived parlimentary regime in 1946, which was soon overthrown by the communists. Maniu was arrested, convicted of being a CIA agent, and died in prison.

Historical programming has been dealt with from time to time by RFE/RL, but a more consistent and comprehensive approach, perhaps utilizing the talents of eminent historians on a freelance basis, should be considered.

SPECIAL PROBLEMS OF RADIO LIBERTY

In covering history and other subjects, Radio Liberty's Russian language service has special responsibilities and concerns not faced by the other services. The Russian service covers the largest and most diverse population of any of the Radios, as well as the core group of any effort to influence minds in the communist world. In addition, this population does not share as many close historical or philosophical ties with the West as Eastern European audiences. There is a question as to the extent to which Radio Liberty's broadcasts should attempt to actively persuade this large population of the value of Western parlimentary democracy. To oversimplify somewhat, there are two schools of thought among the Russian emigré community. The first school includes many of the earlier emigrés who came out before or just after World War II. This group is associated with the prerevolutionary Russian traditions, the Orthodox Church, and the virtues of charity, love of family, and so forth. They have a respect for individual rights and human freedom but are not all totally convinced that the Russian people are ready for parliamentary democracy. Some members of this emigré group, called the "neo-slavophiles," say that an old Russian tradition that is more suitable for them than parliamentary democracy is the town assembly or *Veche*, somewhat similar to a New England Town Meeting. Major decisions for the town would be made at this meeting.

The second group includes a large proportion of more recent emigrés. In general, they are more in favor of parliamentary democracy and other institutions of the Western world. They are less concerned about religion, though they regard religious freedom as a fundamental human right. Known as the "democrats," their leading hero is Andrei Sakharov, who as of this writing is still in the Soviet Union, exiled in Gorky. There is some contention among those interested in broadcsting policy as to which route Radio Liberty should take, if it receives the appropriations requested to enlarge its services.

It seems evident that Radio Liberty could cover both points of view adequately, as they are not necessarily contradictory. Any broadcast service to the U.S.S.R. would be incomplete without religious programming, and traditional Russian values should be prominently featured in historical discussions and other airings. On the other hand, an American station cannot ignore discussions on the values of parliamentary democracy. If a large group in the Russian emigré community espouses this point of view, their opinions should be given an ample outlet.

Radio Liberty would not be urging the population of Russia to revolt, or to attempt to install either of the above systems of government. An independent radio simply provides a platform for diverse points of view. It is expected that in airing such views efficiently Radio Liberty is performing a valuable service for the people of Russia, the general population as well as the elites, by offering alternative views from those of the central Soviet government and press.

Almost all recent emigrés from the Soviet Union are from the second group, the "democrats," and generally are the younger generation. Thus most recent recruits for Radio Liberty have emerged from this school of thought. As a result, the proportion of Radio Liberty personnel from the "neo-slavophile" group has been declining. The younger recruits have the advantage of having lived in Russia more recently and thus are more familiar with current problems within the country, as well as the latest language usage. But they have been criticized for having less familiarity with Western thinking and the literature of democracy because of their restricted education in the Soviet Union, in spite of their dedication to democracy. For example, it has been said that they are more apt to divide everyone into either friends or enemies, "them" or "us," and to consider Western habits of tolerance for different points of view as weakness or political indifference.[27]

These recent emigrés, newly recruited to Radio Liberty, have less interest in airing program appealing to traditional Russian values. Another factor discouraging Radio Liberty from broadcasts on traditional Russian themes is the residual effects of a highly negative report on Radio Liberty programming issued by the BIB in early 1981. This criticized several Radio Liberty broadcasts for being "anti-democratic," "anti-semitic," and "pan-slavic."[28]

The management of RFE/RL responded by calling the BIB report inaccurate and unfair. This was one of the most serious contentions between the BIB and the RFE/RL management before the two boards were merged in 1982. Although RFE/RL management denied the accusations, the aftermath left Radio Liberty more cautious about airing traditional Russian themes. In the opinion of one commentator, this plus the increase in newer emigrés on the staff has resulted in a low percentage of RL broadcasts of special interest to ethnic Russians.[29]

RFE/RL management also should examine another major question involving Radio Liberty: the wisdom of having merged its newsroom into the RFE newsroom in 1976. This decision has been criticized by some Radio Liberty veterans as having undermined the effectiveness of Radio Liberty news, as described earlier. A separate Radio Liberty newsroom could do much to enhance the effectiveness of news broadcasts to the U.S.S.R. and might contribute towards increasing its presently low audience coverage, now running at around 6 percent.

Under the former system, items selected from the total news wire for their interest to Russian listeners were then *rewritten completely in Russian* by the newswriters, if necessary elaborating on the original material, producing more effective copy than the nearly word-for-word translation required by the present language services of RFE.

Previous experience of the international media has shown that direct translations of text are much less effective than the original version. Such word-for-word translations can lose most of the literary merit or journalistic vigor of the original. The solution is to have the text completely rewritten by a good writer in the new language. *Time, Life,* and the *Reader's Digest,* for example, discovered this in launching their international magazines after World War II. *Life* had to hire a group of outstanding Latin American journalists to rewrite *Life* from scratch in producing *Life En Español. Time* never got off the ground in publishing a magazine that would duplicate "Time Style" in Spanish. A direct translation into Spanish simply came out as dry news fodder.

Radio Liberty also broadcasts in 14 other languages to reach the various regions of the Soviet Union. In most cases the English news for these languages now has to be translated *first into Russian* and then into Azeri, Uzbek, Latvian, and so on. If this news output appeared directly in Russian, the extra expense might be offset by not having to translate it first from English before translating into these other languages.

It should be noted that although a separate Radio Liberty news operation would improve its performance, it would also rekindle another problem that surfaced during its previous, independent history: the tendency of the Great Russian majority in the RL management to dominate the other language groups. This created tensions, especially with the Ukrainians, Byelorussians, and Baltic nationals. These emigrés were apprehensive about what they perceived to be a Russian propensity to neglect the sentiments for national survival among other nationalities. For this reason, the establishment of an independent Radio Liberty newsroom should include a representative of senior management, probably a non-Russian, to ensure that the interests of the non-Russian groups are preserved.[30]

OTHER RECOMMENDATIONS

Cuba, Vietnam, and East Germany

A truly effective and meaningful information campaign aimed at the promotion of democratization should also include "surrogate home services" for other major areas where the Soviet Union is deeply involved. The aim would be to provide functions not falling within the VOA Charter. In particular, Cuba and Vietnam would be crucial targets in an information offensive.

As outlined earlier, plans are underway for a service to Cuba, entitled Radio Marti, after the famous Cuban patriot. An internal memorandum from C. Rodney Smith, former Director of RFE, to the Radio Marti Advisory Committee suggests some of the requirements for this service:

It goes without saying that the political commentary...should be low key, invariably accurate, and presented so as to appeal to the important parts of the Cuban audience, and especially not to antagonize them or cause them to feel that the Yankee is trying to "use" them. To achieve this goal of saying the right kind of message at the right time, it is absolutely essential that the station have a research and analysis group of well qualified people knowledgeable about Cuba and Cubans, with monitoring of Cuban broadcasts and media, so as to know accurately exactly what the Cuban government regime is telling the people, and especially what it is not telling.

It would be a serious mistake to put on the air any Cuban political exiles who would harangue their compatriots and oratorically rail against Castro. Able, serious, competent Cuban exiles should be on the staff and will be invaluable for their insight into Cuban verities.

This Cuban broadcasting effort is intended to serve the same sort of purpose as RFE/RL, not duplicate the equally important but very different VOA broadcasting. In short, it should be a station of and for the Cuban people, with broadcasts of direct interest to them, and clearly speaking in their behalf. The Cuban people should know that they can depend upon the station speaking in their interests, on behalf of a free Cuba; at the same time, it should dispel false things the Castro regime says about the U.S. and the free world generally. It should be a station they can stay tuned to and enjoy, as well as be accurately informed. As the Polish RFE station found out, a little thing like regularly giving the local weather forecast, made an amazingly favorable impression, created a feeling that this was really their own local station. . . .[31]

A bill authorizing this service passed the House in 1982 but was held up in the Senate by the threat of filibuster. It was reintroduced in the Senate again in 1983. After some further delays, a compromise bill passed in September 1983, which placed the new Cuban service under the Voice of America. This arrangement would seem to inhibit the objectives of providing a surrogate home service for the Cuban people because of the limitations of the Voice charter. But the compromise bill includes detailed provisions placing the new Radio in a special division of the Voice, with its own personnel and its own Director reporting to the Director of the Voice and the USIA. A sponsor of the bill, Senator Paula Hawkins (R-Fla.), said on the Senate floor that "under this amendment Radio Marti can provide credible, reliable information and programs similar to those broadcast by Radio Free Europe and Radio Liberty. Radio Marti can serve as a 'surrogate home service' for the Cuban people." Senator Charles Percy followed Senator Hawkins on the floor and said that the new Radio's "most important mission will be to act as a surrogate home service for Cuban citizens who are unable to obtain such service from their own media."[32]

Vietnam is also an important nation with strong Soviet involvement. It now has a population of 57 million people and is the most aggressive state in Southeast Asia. A surrogate home service for this country could give the large population, especially in the south, local news not available on VOA, and commentaries to enable them to preserve the hope that they are not being abandoned by the outside world. VOA is already broadcasting international news in Vietnamese and transmits information about the Vietnamese community in the United States, as for example, activities in preserving the Vietnamese folk music tradition.

The emigrés from Vietnam now include a large number of outstanding musicians. The country has a long tradition of vigorous folk music, which has been almost wiped out by the communist regime. A large community of Vietnamese emigré musicians in California is continuing this tradition, composing new music, and establishing a new center for Vietnamese music. This group includes La Thaoi Tan, once one of the most popular musicians and comedians in his country, known as "the Bob Hope of Vietnam."

The Voice of America performs some of these services, but it does not attempt to cover local news or, for example, news of the Vietnamese soldiers serving in Cambodia and Laos. It broadcasts only three hours daily.

A Vietnamese "surrogate home service" could be part of a revived Radio Free Asia. As noted in Chapter 2, the original RFA was established in 1951 to broadcast to Mainland China but was discontinued in 1953 during the major budget cuts in all information services.

East Germany is an important area not covered by the Voice of America. It is reached by RIAS (Radio in the American Sector), described earlier. West Germany is now providing the bulk of the financing for RIAS, but the station continues to operate under the supervision of American management reporting to USIA. The service has lost some of its audience now that the East Germans have more access to other Western radio and television stations from West Germany, Austria, and Switzerland. But RIAS still reaches an estimated 40 percent of the East German people and remains the only free world station that concentrates on news and features about East Germany itself.[33] As such, RIAS should remain a high-priority service for continuation in an activist international broadcasting strategy.

FURTHER RECOMMENDATIONS

The following are additional recommendations that have been
proposed in the broadcasting community that should also be
considered:

(1) America's information strategy is so important a part of
our overall strategy that it requires more coordination than it
has received up to now. At present, piecemeal direction is provided by the State Department, the National Security Council,
the White House, and Congress. VOA and RIAS report to
USIA, which is responsible to the President, taking policy
guidance from the State Department. RFE/RL is governed by
the BIB, which is required to report annually to the President
and Congress and is provided by the Secretary of State with
"such information regarding the foreign policy of the United
States as the Secretary may deem appropriate." The effort requires overall direction from one official, perhaps an Assistant
Secretary of State for Public Diplomacy.

Such an individual, supported by an appropriate staff,
would not only coordinate the work of our international
broadcast agencies, but also would advise all departments of
the government on affairs relating to public opinion overseas.
This official would serve as an advisor to the National Security
Council and as principal advisor to the President on matters
of foreign public opinion and the conduct of public diplomacy. Not since Edward R. Murrow in the Kennedy Administration has one offical performed all these functions.

(2) Broadcasting, and America's information program as a
whole, are of great importance in the ongoing contest with the
communists for public opinion in the world. The program requires the services of the finest minds in this country in the
areas of information, communications, the arts of persuasion,
and on the Soviet theory and practice of propaganda. Many
able men and women are serving in our broadcasting agencies,
but a more vigorous recruiting effort is needed, particularly
recruitment of talent for experts in the arts of persuasion and
on communist propaganda. In any effort to win the minds of

the people of the communist countries, it is not enough to give them straight news embellished with features on the virtues of free institutions. The communists have been constructing an edifice of propaganda for decades to answer and offset the points that free people may raise in attempting to persuade other people of the advantages of free enterprise and liberal democracy. Such an effort requires experts knowledgeable about this Soviet propaganda lexicon to be able to speak against it effectively.

(3) Jamming is an issue that demands the coordination of broadcasting with the broader concerns of diplomacy. For nearly four decades the Soviets have been jamming Western broadcasts on a massive scale, in direct violation of the UN Declaration on Human Rights and the Helsinki Agreement. And yet the issue has elicited relatively weak protests from the United States and the other Western nations. This should be made a major issue in all future negotiations with the Soviets, as well as in international forums.

Up to now the Soviets have claimed that Western broadcasts represent an interference in their internal affairs, although their own foreign broadcasts are much more virulent. Every major negotiation with the Soviets, including new grain deals, new trade treaties, agreements on cultural exchanges, or arms control, should deal with the issue of jamming. Our Western allies should be urged to treat the problem with more gravity then they have in the past. Such pressure might bring some results, but even if reductions in jamming are slight, world opinion would be more aware of this continuing violation of the UN Declaration of Human Rights and the Helsinki Agreement.

(4) Our NATO allies should also be urged to do more in broadcasting, especially to the Soviet Union, and particularly to the non-Russian republics. Radio Liberty broadcasts in 14 languages of the Soviet Republics other than Russian and VOA broadcasts in seven. The BBC, in contrast, uses only Russian and English. Deutsche Welle broadcasts to the Soviet Union only in Russian and German and Kol Israel in Yiddish and

Hebrew. More should be done on the diplomatic front to persuade our allies to carry a heavier portion of the broadcast burden to the U.S.S.R.

(5) Although VOA and the Radios have often been a subject of intense interest to many in Congress and the Government, as well as to crusaders with varying points of view in the media, they are scarcely known to the American public. The Voice is prohibited by law from disseminating its output within the United States. The American people should be told more about these organizations, as greater public awareness would undoubtedly increase public support for the Radios in Congress.

One instrument for promoting greater knowledge could be the Radio Free Europe/Radio Liberty Fund. This is a private nonprofit corporation that evolved from the Crusade for Freedom, a fundraising effort launched by the National Committee for a Free Europe in 1950. When the Radios were taken out from under this organization and put under the Board for International Broadcasting in 1974, the RFE/RL Fund was continued as a private organization for raising money from foundations, corporations, and individuals to support projects paralleling the activities of the Radios that do not come under specific government funding authorizations. Like the Crusade for Freedom in the 1950s, a public information campaign about our international radio activities could be a successful and valuable effort for this organization.

(6) International broadcasting should be part of a bipartisan effort in the United States along with its allies as outlined in President Reagan's speech before the British Parliament in June 1982. The American Political Foundation, a bipartisan organization in Washington, D.C., has been making a study of how U.S. public and private organizations can contribute to a global campaign for democracy. Their interim report, issued in April 1983, recommended activities by American labor unions, business, and both major political parties to work with their opposite numbers in other countries to promote democracy. The program would work through five organizations:

The Democratic and Republican Political Foundations to coordinate the work of both parties, similar to foundations organized by political parties in Western Europe to support democratic movements in other countries;

The Free Trade Union Institute, an organization formed by the AFL/CIO in 1978 to assist the growth of free trade unions in other countries;

The Center for International Private Enterprise, to work initially with the U.S. Chamber of Commerce to encourage the growth of private enterprise abroad "as a necessary element of democratic pluralism";

A National Endowment for Democracy as a permanent coordinator of the project.[34]

Much of this work, and in particular the efforts of labor and private enterprise foundations, could be of value in coordination with American broadcasting efforts into the communist countries. Advisers to the Center for International Private Enterprise, for example, are considering a proposal for encouraging "employee-owned enterprises" that might have some appeal in broadcasts to communist countries. This form of worker-ownership of firms has many advantages over so-called collective ownership, where the worker in fact has little real control and no ownership stake.[35]

The AFL-CIO has been active for decades in a campaign to support free labor unions in other countries and to combat the efforts of communists to destroy them. Among the objectives of the Free Trade Union Institute under the new Democracy Project will be "aid to the efforts to organize independent unions in communist countries." The labor advisors to the project say that support for those attempting to establish free unions in communist countries can come only on initiatives from within such countries. "The shape and size of such efforts are totally dependent on the initiative and requirements of those making the request for help . . . . there exists the unprecedented challenge to the imagination of free trade unionists of Solidarity's attempt to organize an independent union in a communist country. Although this attempt met with violent repression, the Solidarity experience may foreshadow possible future events elsewhere in the communist world of deep interest and concern to democratic trade unionists."[36]

Congress now has under consideration this report and budget proposals totalling $31 million for the five foundations. These activities would furnish important material for broadcasts into the communist countries.

As President Reagan concluded before the British Parliament in June 1982, there is a "global campaign for democracy now gathering force. For the ultimate determinant in the struggle now going on in the world will not be bombs or rockets, but test of wills, a test of spiritual resolve, the values we have, the beliefs we cherish, the ideas to which we are dedicated. For the sake of peace and justice let us move toward a world in which all people are at last free to determine their own destiny."

NOTES

1. Interviews with VOA, RFE/RL, State Department and National Security Council personnel, and Congressional staffers.
2. Interviews with RFE/RL officials in Washington D.C., September 1983.
3. For example, in the Media Institute panel discussion on VOA cited earlier, three out of the four panelists (Philip Nicolaides, Bernard Kamenske, and Jozsef Takacs) recommended that FSIOs be phased out or not given senior roles and that VOA be taken out from under USIA. The fourth panelist, M. William Haratunian, is himself a member of the Foreign Service.
4. For example, a VOA "Vacancy Announcement" of January 18, 1983 posted on the VOA bulletin boards shows that an opening for an International Radio Broadcaster (Foreign Language) is ranked from GS5 to GS11, while four openings for International Radio Broadcasters (English) are ranked GS11 or GS12.
5. Interviews with RL language desk writers and editors in Munich.
6. George P. Shultz, "U.S.-Soviet Foreign Relations in the Context of U.S. Foreign Policy," Statement before the Senate Foreign Relations Committee, June 15, 1983, Washington D.C., Department of State, No. 213.
7. Interview with a Voice editor.
8. VOA estimates as of March 1983. Document #1426E.
9. Madame Chiang Kai Shek, *Conversations with Mikhail Borodin*, (Taipei: Government Information Office, 1976), p. 24.

10. See, for example, memorandum by Lev Navrozov, *Intellectual Level, Content, and Effectiveness of Radio Liberty*, 2/28/77. (Internal memo).

11. John Lenzcowski, *Soviet Perceptions of U.S. Foreign Policy*, (Ithaca: Cornell University Press, 1982), pp. 27–30, and 239.

12. Interview with violinist Albert Markov.

13. A Hungarian desk man in Munich said in a recent interview that in many cases RFE is engaging in "self-jamming" by broadcasting an excessive amount of pop music.

14. East European Bible Mission, *Newsletter*, Roosendahl, The Netherlands, 2/79.

15. Sabur, p. 7.

16. This failing in Soviet science is summarized in an as yet unpublished manuscript by Dr. Lawrence Cranberg, a consulting physicist in Austin, Texas, entitled "Detour to Dystopia", a history of Marxist theory and its relation to science, Chapter 43.

17. Dr. Walter Reich, "The World of Soviet Psychiatry," *N.Y. Times Magazine*, January 30, 1983, pp. 21 ff.

18. *UN Demographic Yearbook*, 1979, passim.

19. Interview with Polish emigré who prefers to remain anonymous.

20. "The Woman and Russia," *Freedom Appeals*, May-June 1980, (Freedom House, New York), pp. 3–12.

21. Radio Liberty, "Trend Report — Radio Liberty's Audience in the USSR," April 1982, p. 13. RFE, "Listening to Western Radio in East Europe," June, 1982, p. 10.

22. Radio Liberty Audience Research Department, "Attitudes of Byelorussians," 5/81.

23. *Soviet World Outlook*, Volume 7, number 8. August 15, 1982. Published by the Advanced International Studies Institute, Inc.

24. See note 19. These comments on Soviet strategy should be considered the testimony of one man, which has been disputed by other authorities.

25. Interviews at Committee for Free Afghanistan, Washington. D.C., April 1983.

26. RFE Audience Research Panel Report, 6/81, p. 6.

27. Memo to RFE/RL Management from Dr. Maurice Friedman, January 10, 1979 on "Radio Liberty Programming for Period of May 25 to June 1, 1978."

28. BIB Report, "Review of Radio Liberty Russian Service Broadcasts," Washington, D.C., January 29, 1981; Memo from Dr. Glenn W. Ferguson, President, RFE/RL to Board of Directors, RFE/RL, "BIB Review of Radio Liberty Russian Service Broadcasts," April 13, 1981.

29. Interview by the author with a Russian emigré recently appointed to a senior position in Radio Liberty, August 11, 1983.
30. This point was raised in a letter to RFE/RL Management signed by eight faculty members of the Ukrainian Free University in Munich and nine other scholars and members of Ukrainian emigré groups in Western Europe, dated May 25, 1982. It was also mentioned by Waclaw Melianovich, a representative of the Byelorussian community in the United States, in an interview with the author on June 5, 1983.
31. C. Rodney Smith memo of February 1, 1982.
32. Congressional Record, September 13, 1983, pp. S12076,12077.
33. Browne, pp. 134, 135.
34. *The Commitment to Democracy: A Bipartisan Approach,* (Washington, D.C.: The American Political Foundation, April 18, 1983), pp. 17–43.
35. Dr. Norman Kurland, "Employee-Owned Enterprises", speech at conference, "Striving for Freedom", of the Association for Cooperation of Democratic Countries, Washington, D.C., May 6, 1983.
36. *Commitment to Democracy,* pp. 39, 40.

APPENDICES

Annual Budgets, RFE/RL & VOA
Actual & Constant 1972 Dollars (Millions)

| | RFE/RL | | VOA | |
| | Actual | Constant 1972 | Actual | Constant 1972 |
Fiscal Year	Dollars	Dollars	Dollars	Dollars
1949	-	-	6.9	14.9
1950	3.1	6.6	8.9	19.1
1951	8.7	17.8	13.1	26.9
1952	17.0	32.6	19.8	38.0
1953	17.3	32.4	21.7	40.6
1954	14.9	31.6	14.5	30.7
1955	14.5	26.6	15.5	28.4
1956	15.9	28.3	16.9	30.1
1957	19.8	33.6	20.3	34.5
1958	15.6	28.4	17.1	27.8
1959	19.8	31.3	18.0	28.4
1960	20.9	32.6	17.4	27.2
1961	20.4	31.2	18.1	27.6
1962	21.1	31.7	19.8	29.8
1963	22.8	33.4	23.2	33.9
1964	25.6	36.7	27.1	38.9
1965	26.6	37.5	28.1	39.6
1966	27.2	36.9	30.1	40.8
1967	26.4	34.7	31.8	41.8
1968	29.0	36.5	32.9	41.4
1969	32.3	38.8	35.8	43.0
1970	32.8	36.8	39.3	44.2

Appendix I (*continued*)
Annual Budgets, RFE/RL & VOA
Actual & Constant 1972 Dollars (Millions)

| | RFE/RL | | VOA | |
Fiscal Year	Actual Dollars	Constant 1972 Dollars	Actual Dollars	Constant 1972 Dollars
1971	33.7	35.6	41.6	44.0
1972	32.9	32.9	45.5	45.5
1973	39.7	37.6	49.0	46.5
1974	49.5	43.7	52.3	46.2
1975	49.5*	39.7	56.9	45.7
1976	64.1**	48.3	59.9	45.2
1977	52.7	37.0	65.5	45.9
1978	67.3	44.2	69.5	45.6
1979	78.0	47.3	75.1	45.6
1980	80.4	44.5	85.4	47.2
1981	97.5	49.8	96.0	48.3
1982	82.4	38.4	116.1	54.2
1983 Est.	89.4	N.A.	117.2	N.A.
1984 Est.	103.6	N.A.	N.A.	N.A.

Constant dollar conversion factors were obtained from the Office of Management and Budget.

* From 1975 to date the RFE/RL budgets were heavily influenced by fluctuations in the dollar/mark exchange rate since a high proportion of expenses are in Germany.
** The 1976 RFE/RL budget is high because of a change in the fiscal year and the merger between RFE and RL.

Appendix II
Available Employment Statistics—RFE/RL & VOA

	RFE	RL	Total RFE/RL	VOA
1955	-	-	-	649
1960	-	-	-	1,616
1963	-	909	-	-
1964	-	1,006	-	-
1965	-	1,092	-	2,248
1966	-	1,107	-	-
1967	-	1,084	-	-
1968	1,793	1,042	2,835	-
1969	1,723	1,035	2,762	-
1970	1,665	1,027	2,692	2,310
1971	1,637	1,004	2,641	-
1972	1,485	896	2,381	-
1973	1,515	853	2,368	-
1974	1,247	778	2,025	-
1975	1,258	753	2,011	2,263
1976	-	-	1,821	-
1977	-	-	1,765	-
1978	-	-	1,749	-
1979	-	-	1,730	-
1980	-	-	1,664	2,200
1981	-	-	1,666	-
1982	-	-	1,674	2,300

Since VOA did not have its own personnel department until 1982, figures are not conveniently available for every year. The available figures do indicate the trends.

The 1982 VOA figure does not include employees of the USICA Television and Film Service, which became part of the Broadcasting Directorate in May 1982.

James L. Tyson has spent most of his career in the fields of International Communications or Economics. He graduated from Harvard in History and Economics. During World War II he served in the Navy, assigned to the Office of Strategic Services as an economist in England and Italy. From 1946 to 1959 he was Research Director of Time-Life International in charge of Economic and Public Opinion Research for those publications. He was a founding member of the World Association of Public Opinion Research. From 1964 to 1982 he was with the IBM World Trade Corporation. He is now a consultant with Accuracy in Media, Inc. in Washington, D. C. He is the author of *Target America — The Influence of Communist Propaganda on U.S. Media* and has written articles on International Affairs and Economics published in *Fortune, Barron's, Asian Affairs,* and *Dun's International Markets,* and distributed by United Features and the North American Newspaper Alliance.

ACKNOWLEDGMENTS

I would like to acknowledge the assistance of Sara Begley, formerly a graduate student at Georgetown University, and Glenn Kessler, formerly a graduate student at the Columbia University School of International Affairs in the research of this study. Many present and former officers and staff of the Voice of America and Radio Free Europe/Radio Liberty in Munich, New York, and Washington were also of great help, as well as several people in the U.S. Information Agency, the State Department, and the National Security Council. Since many requested anonymity, it seemed best not to list them individually. A number of Americans of Eastern European or Russian backgrounds also provided valuable suggestions, including Stephen Gereben of the Coordinating Committee of Hungarian Organizations, Katherine Chumachenko of the Ukrainian Congress Committee of America, Waclaw Melianovich of the Byelorussian-American Association, Dr. Igor Glagolev of the Association for Cooperation of Democratic Countries, Ian Nowak, and Lev Navrozov. Several Americans with experience in senior positions in U.S. international information activities also provided valuable advice, including especially General C. Rodney Smith, Donald Dunham, and Kenneth Giddens.

153

National Strategy Information Center, Inc.

PUBLICATIONS

Gerald L. Steibel, Editor
Joyce E. Larson, Associate Editor   William C. Bodie, Associate Editor

STRATEGY PAPERS

The Soviet Control Structure: Capabilities for Wartime Survival by Harriet
Fast Scott and William F. Scott, September 1983

Strategic Weapons: An Introduction by Norman Polmar, October 1975. Revised edition, June 1982

Conventional War and Escalation: The Soviet View by Joseph D. Douglass,
Jr. and Amoretta M. Hoeber, November 1981

*Soviet Perceptions of Military Doctrine and Military Power: The Interaction
of Theory and Practice* by John J. Dziak, June 1981

How Little is Enough? SALT and Security in the Long Run by Francis P.
Hoeber, January 1981

Raw Material Supply in a Multipolar World by Yuan-li Wu, October 1973.
Revised edition, October 1979

India: Emergent Power? by Stephen P. Cohen and Richard L. Park, June
1978

The Kremlin and Labor: A Study in National Security Policy by Roy Godson, November 1977

The Evolution of Soviet Security Strategy 1965-1975 by Avigdor Haselkorn,
November 1977

The Geopolitics of the Nuclear Era by Colin S. Gray, September 1977

The Sino-Soviet Confrontation: Implications for the Future by Harold C.
Hinton, September 1976 (Out of print)

Food, Foreign Policy, and Raw Materials Cartels by William Schneider, Jr.,
February 1976

Soviet Sources of Military Doctrine and Strategy by William F. Scott, July
1975

Detente: Promises and Pitfalls by Gerald L. Steibel, March 1975 (Out of
print)

Oil, Politics and Sea Power: The Indian Ocean Vortex by Ian W. A. C.
Adie, December 1974 (Out of print)

The Soviet Presence in Latin America by James D. Theberge, June 1974

The Horn of Africa by J. Bowyer Bell, Jr., December 1973

Research and Development and the Prospects for International Security by
Frederick Seitz and Rodney W. Nichols, December 1973

The People's Liberation Army: Communist China's Armed Forces by Angus
M. Fraser, August 1973 (Out of print)

The China Sea: The American Stake in its Future by Harold C. Hinton, January 1981

NATO, Turkey, and the Southern Flank: A Mideastern Perspective by Ihsan Gürkan, March 1980

The Soviet Threat to NATO's Northern Flank by Marian K. Leighton, November 1979

Does Defense Beggar Welfare? Myths Versus Realities by James L. Clayton, June 1979 (Out of print)

Naval Race or Arms Control in the Indian Ocean? (Some Problems in Negotiating Naval Limitations) by Alvin Cottrell and Walter F. Hahn, September 1978 (Out of print)

Power Projection: A Net Assessment of U.S. and Soviet Capabilities by W. Scott Thompson, April 1978

Understanding the Soviet Military Threat, How CIA Estimates Went Astray by William T. Lee, February 1977 (Out of print)

Toward a New Defense for NATO, The Case for Tactical Nuclear Weapons, July 1976 (Out of print)

Seven Tracks to Peace in the Middle East by Frank R. Barnett, April 1975

Arms Treaties with Moscow: Unequal Terms Unevenly Applied? by Donald G. Brennan, April 1975 (Out of print)

Toward a U.S. Energy Policy by Klaus Knorr, March 1975 (Out of print)

Can We Avert Economic Warfare in Raw Materials? US Agriculture as a Blue Chip by William Schneider, Jr., July 1974

BOOKS

On the Brink: Defense, Deficits, and Welfare Spending by James L. Clayton, November 1983

U.S. International Broadcasting and National Security by James L. Tyson, November 1983

Arms, Men, and Military Budgets: Issues for Fiscal Year 1981 by Francis P. Hoeber, William Schneider, Jr., Norman Polmar, and Ray Bessette, May 1980

Arms, Men, and Military Budgets: Issues for Fiscal Year 1979 by Francis P. Hoeber, David B. Kassing, and William Schneider, Jr., February 1978

Arms, Men, and Military Budgets: Issues for Fiscal Year 1978 edited by Francis P. Hoeber and William Schneider, Jr., May 1977

Arms, Men, and Military Budgets: Issues for Fiscal Year 1977 edited by William Schneider, Jr., and Francis P. Hoeber, May 1976

* * *

Intelligence Requirements for the 1980s: Clandestine Collection (Volume V of a Series) edited by Roy Godson, November 1982

Intelligence Requirements for the 1980s: Covert Action (Volume IV of a Series) edited by Roy Godson, September 1981

Intelligence Requirements for the 1980s: Counterintelligence (Volume III of a Series) edited by Roy Godson, January 1981

Intelligence Requirements for the 1980s: Analysis and Estimates (Volume II of a Series) edited by Roy Godson, June 1980

Intelligence Requirements for the 1980s: Elements of Intelligence (Volume I of a Series) edited by Roy Godson, October 1979

* * *

The Soviet View of U.S. Strategic Doctrine by Jonathan Samuel Lockwood, April 1983

Strategic Military Surprise: Incentives and Opportunities edited by Klaus Knorr and Patrick Morgan, January 1983

National Security Affairs: Theoretical Perspectives and Contemporary Issues edited by B. Thomas Trout and James E. Harf, October 1982

False Science: Underestimating the Soviet Arms Buildup by Steven Rosefielde, July 1982

Our Changing Geopolitical Premises by Thomas P. Rona, January 1982

Strategic Minerals: A Resource Crisis published by the Council on Economics and National Security (an NSIC Project), December 1981

U.S. Policy and Low-Intensity Conflict: Potentials for Military Struggles in the 1980s edited by Sam C. Sarkesian and William L. Scully, June 1981

New Foundations for Asian and Pacific Security edited by Joyce E. Larson, September 1980

The Fateful Ends and Shades of SALT: Past . . . Present . . . And Yet to Come? by Paul H. Nitze, James E. Dougherty, and Francis X. Kane, March 1979

Strategic Options for the Early Eighties: What Can Be Done? edited by William R. Van Cleave and W. Scott Thompson, February 1979

Oil, Divestiture and National Security edited by Frank N. Trager, December 1976 (Out of print)

Indian Ocean Naval Limitations, Regional Issues and Global Implications by Alvin J. Cottrell and Walter F. Hahn, April 1976

* * *

The Intelligent Layperson's Guide to the Nuclear Freeze and Peace Debate by Joyce E. Larson and William C. Bodie, March 1983
War and Peace: Soviet Russia Speaks edited by Albert L. Weeks and William C. Bodie, with an essay by Frank R. Barnett, March 1983

The National Strategy Information Center is a non-partisan tax-exempt institution organized in 1962 to conduct educational programs in international security affairs.

The Center espouses no political causes. Its Directors and Officers represent a wide spectrum of responsible political opinion from liberal to conservative. What unites them, however, is the conviction that neither isolationism nor pacifism can provide realistic solutions to the challenge of 20th century totalitarianism.

NSIC exists to encourage civil-military partnership on the grounds that, in a democracy, informed public opinion is necessary to a viable U.S. defense system capable of protecting the nation's vital interests and assisting other free nations which aspire to independence and self-fulfillment.